SIMPLE JAVA PROGRAMS

DR. S. UMA | DR. M. AMUTHA

Made with ♥ on the Notion Press Platform
www.notionpress.com

DEDICATED TO ALMIGHTY GOD!!

Contents

Preface *vii*

1. Java Installation 1
2. Print Statements And String Operations 6
3. Data Types, Variables, Operators 19
4. Control Flow 32
5. Arrays 42
6. Classes, Inheritance – Super Classes- Sub Classes –protected Members 54
7. Constructors 81
8. Abstract Classes And Methods- Final Methods 109
9. Interfaces 114
10. Inner Classes 122
11. Exceptions 129
12. Streams – Byte Streams And Character Streams 141
13. Multi-threading And Multitasking 165

Preface

Java has plenty of Job Opportunities!!

Java has one of the largest legacy code bases, or collections of source code, of any computer languages in use today.

Java is particularly adaptable since it can be used to build programmes for the web, mobile devices, desktop computers, and other platforms. Additionally, Java has a lot of features that make it very adaptable, like dynamic coding, several security features, platform independence, network-centric architecture, etc.

Java programming is essential in practical applications including financial services, online applications, and Android apps.

The possibilities for what you may create using Java are virtually endless. Java is the (second) most used programming language.

Companies in the technology, government, financial, healthcare, insurance, education, manufacturing, and defence sectors all use Java.

The backend architecture of 90% of Fortune 500 organisations is Java-based. However, many firms experiencing quick growth utilise Java to power their products as well because of its speed and scalability.

Java programmers earn a lot of money.

The Java community is vibrant and active.

Java is resilient.

Java is an accessible language.

You gain a competitive edge by learning Java.

The goal of this book is to make it simple to learn Java by using straightforward programmes. The applications are provided in relation to the Java concepts.

CHAPTER ONE

Java Installation

Java Installation

Some PCs might have Java already installed.

To check if you have Java installed on a Windows PC, search in the start bar for Java or type the following in Command Prompt (cmd.exe):

C:\Users\Your Name>java –version

If Java is installed, you will see something like this (depending on version):

java version "11.0.1" 2018-10-16 LTS
Java(TM) SE Runtime Environment 18.9 (build 11.0.1+13-LTS)
Java HotSpot(TM) 64-Bit Server VM 18.9 (build 11.0.1+13-LTS, mixed mode)

If you do not have Java installed on your computer, you can download it for free at oracle.com.

Note: In this tutorial, we will write Java code in a text editor. However, it is possible to write Java in an Integrated Development Environment, such as IntelliJ IDEA, Netbeans or Eclipse, which are particularly useful when managing larger collections of Java files.

Setup for Windows

To install Java on Windows:

1. Go to "System Properties" (Can be found on Control Panel > System and Security > System > Advanced System Settings)
2. Click on the "Environment variables" button under the "Advanced" tab
3. Then, select the "Path" variable in System variables and click on the "Edit" button
4. Click on the "New" button and add the path where Java is installed, followed by **\bin**. By default, Java is installed in C:\Program Files\Java\jdk-11.0.1 (If nothing else was specified when you installed it). In that case, You will have to add a new path with: **C:\Program Files\Java\jdk-11.0.1\bin**
   Then, click "OK", and save the settings
5. At last, open Command Prompt (cmd.exe) and type **java -version** to see if Java is running on your machine

Step by Step Installation of Java with Images

Step 1

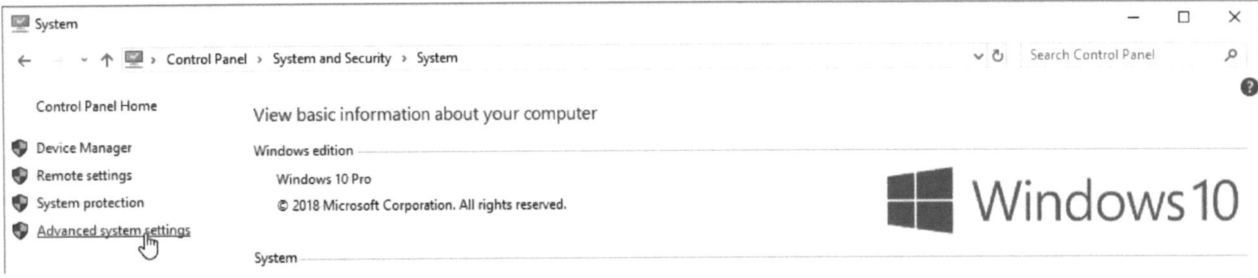
System
Control Panel › System and Security › System
Search Control Panel
Control Panel Home
Device Manager
Remote settings
System protection
Advanced system settings
View basic information about your computer
Windows edition
Windows 10 Pro
© 2018 Microsoft Corporation. All rights reserved.
Windows 10
System

Step 2

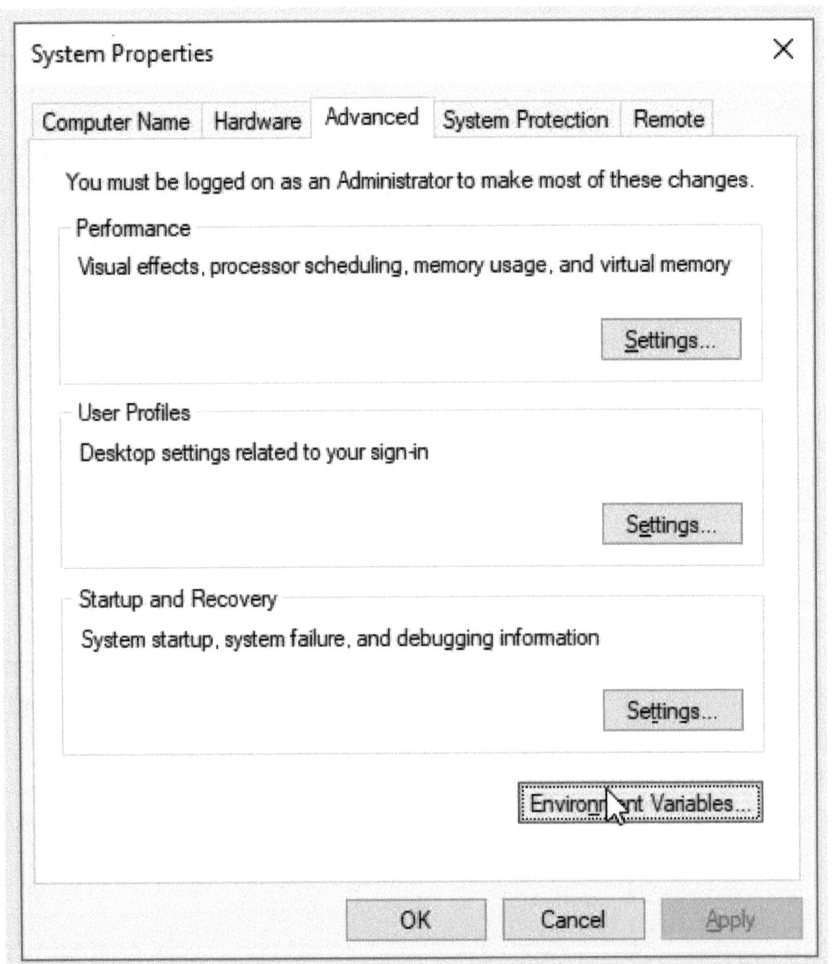
System Properties
Computer Name
Hardware
Advanced
System Protection
Remote
You must be logged on as an Administrator to make most of these changes.
Performance
Visual effects, processor scheduling, memory usage, and virtual memory
Settings...
User Profiles
Desktop settings related to your sign-in
Settings...
Startup and Recovery
System startup, system failure, and debugging information
Settings...
OK
Cancel
Apply

Step 3

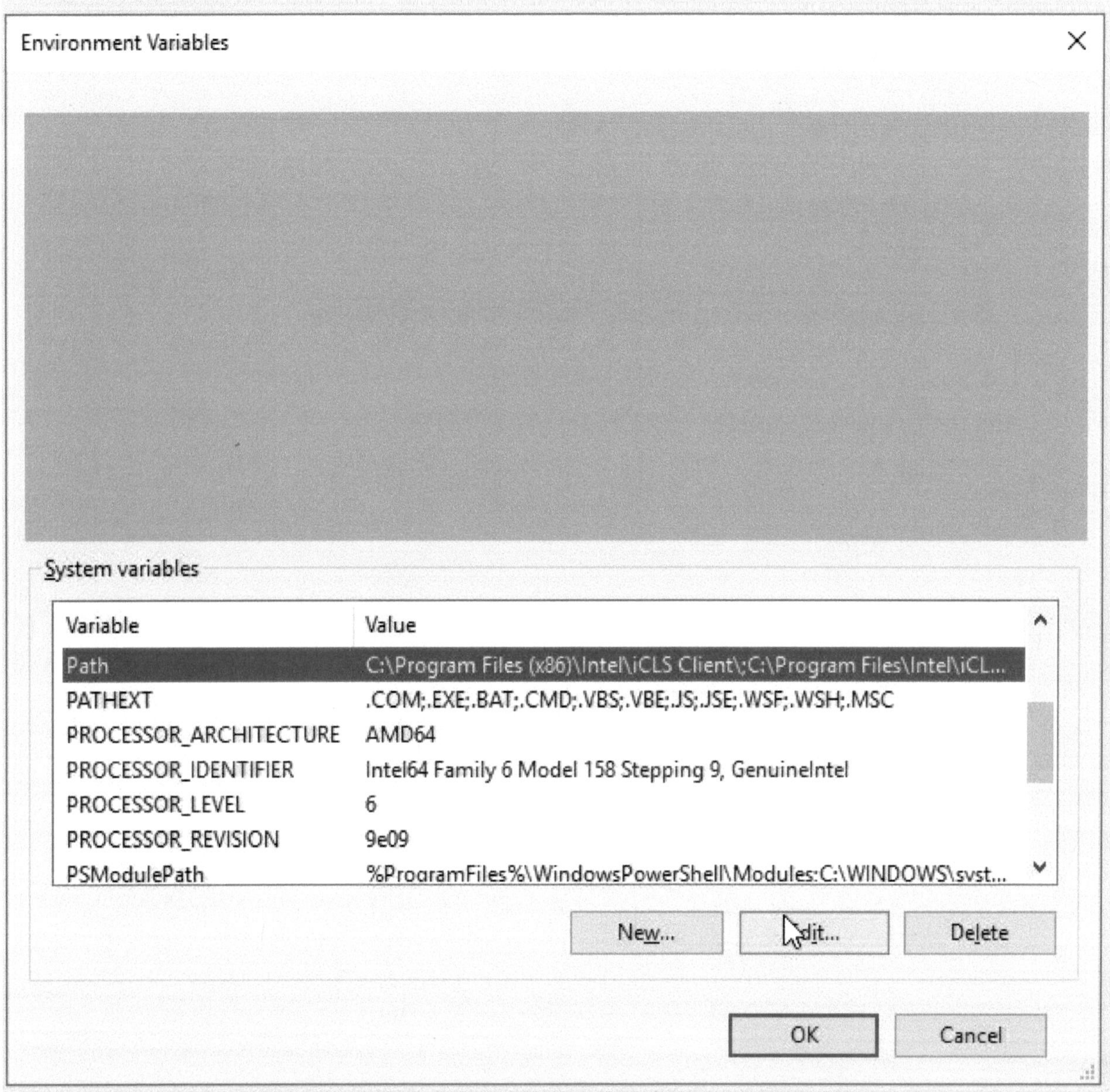
Environment Variables
System variables
Variable
Value
Path
C:\Program Files (x86)\Intel\iCLS Client\;C:\Program Files\Intel\iCL...
PATHEXT
.COM;.EXE;.BAT;.CMD;.VBS;.VBE;.JS;.JSE;.WSF;.WSH;.MSC
PROCESSOR_ARCHITECTURE
AMD64
PROCESSOR_IDENTIFIER
Intel64 Family 6 Model 158 Stepping 9, GenuineIntel
PROCESSOR_LEVEL
6
PROCESSOR_REVISION
9e09
PSModulePath
%ProgramFiles%\WindowsPowerShell\Modules;C:\WINDOWS\syst...
New...
Edit...
Delete
OK
Cancel

Step 4

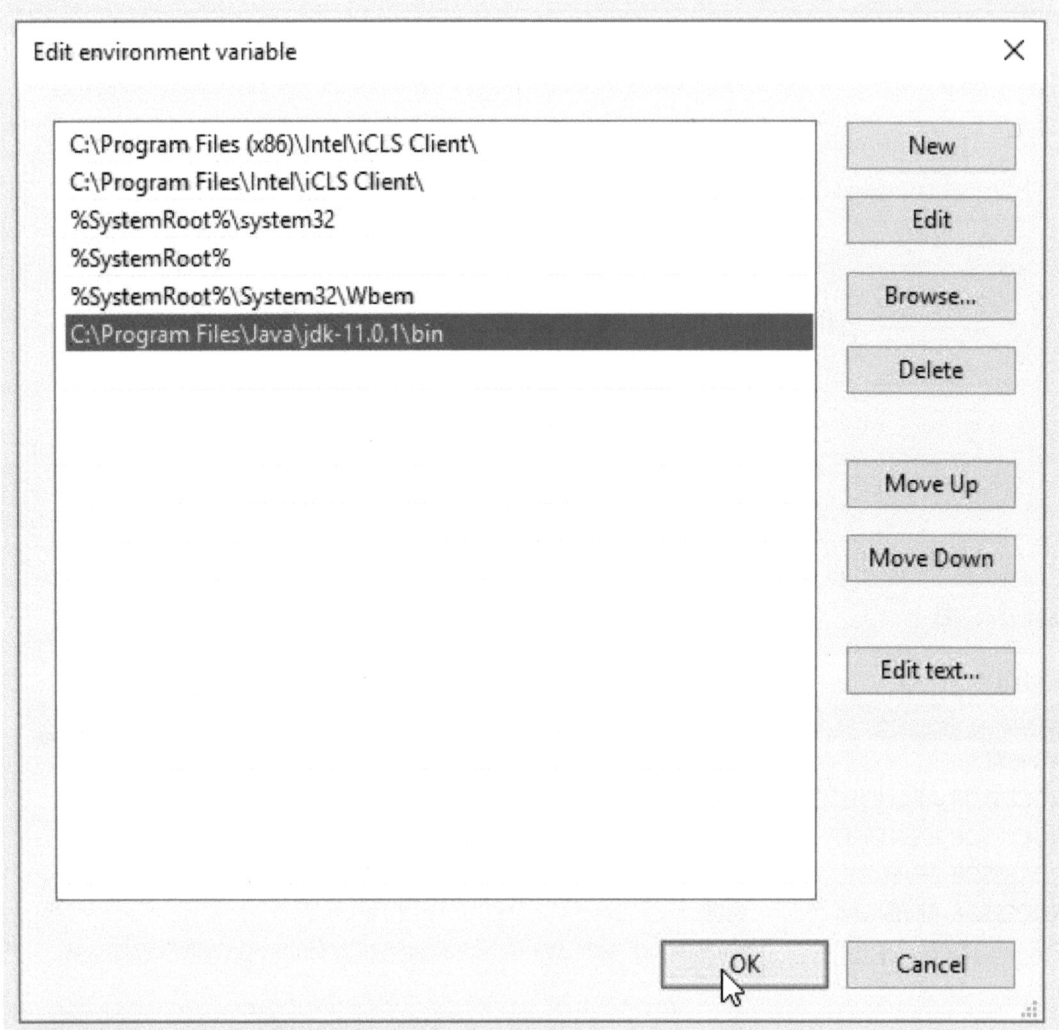

Step 5

Write the following in the command line (cmd.exe):

C:\Users*Your Name*>java -version

If Java was successfully installed, you will see something like this (depending on version):

java version "11.0.1" 2018-10-16 LTS
Java(TM) SE Runtime Environment 18.9 (build 11.0.1+13-LTS)
Java HotSpot(TM) 64-Bit Server VM 18.9 (build 11.0.1+13-LTS, mixed mode)

Quickstart Java

In Java, every application begins with a class name, and that class should match the filename.

Let's create our first Java file, called Sample.java, which can be done in any text editor (like Notepad).

The file contains a "Hello World" message, which is written with the following code:

Sample.java

public class Sample {

```
public static void main(String[] args) {
System.out.println("Hello World!!");
}
}
```

C:\Users\YourName>javac Sample.java

This will compile your code. If there are no errors in the code, the command prompt will take you to the next line. Now, type "java Sample" to run the file:

C:\Users*Your Name*>java Sample

The output is as follows:

Hello World

Every line of code that runs in Java must be inside a class. In our example, we named the class **Sample**. A class should always start with an uppercase first letter.

Note: Java is case-sensitive: "MyClass" and "myclass" has different meaning.

The name of the java file **must match** the class name. When saving the file, save it using the class name and add ".java" to the end of the filename. To run the example above on your computer, make sure that Java is properly installed.The output should be:

Hello World

Explanation:

The main Method

The main() method is required and you will see it in every Java program:

public static void **main**(String[] args)

Any code inside the main() method will be executed. Don't worry about the keywords before and after main.

For now, just remember that every Java program has a class name which must match the filename, and that every program must contain the main() method.

System.out.println()

Inside the main() method, we can use the println() method to print a line of text to the screen:

```
public static void main(String[] args) {
System.out.println("Hello World");
}
```

The curly braces {} marks the beginning and the end of a block of code.

System is a built-in Java class that contains useful members, such as out, which is short for "output". The println() method, short for "print line", is used to print a value to the screen (or a file).

System, out and println()are needed to print any information to the screen.

Each code statement must end with a semicolon (;).

CHAPTER TWO

Print Statements and String Operations

Program: Java Program to print Hello World

```
public class HelloWorld
{
public static void main(String[] args)
{
System.out.println("Hello World");
}
}
```

OUTPUT :

Hello World

Program: Java Program to print some symbols

```
public class PrintPattern
{
public static void main(String[] args)
{
System.out.println("%%%%%");
System.out.println("******");
}
}
```

OUTPUT :

```
%%%%%
******
```

Program: Java Program to print Using println statement

```
//Using println statement
public class Main
{
public static void main(String[] args)
```

```
{
System.out.println("Hello World!");
System.out.println("Welcome to Simple Java Programs");
}
}
```

OUTPUT :

Hello World!
Welcome to Simple Java Programs

Program: Java Program to print Using print statement

```
//Using print statement
public class Main
{
public static void main(String[] args)
{
System.out.print("Hello World!");
System.out.print("Welcome to Simple Java Programs");
}
}
```

OUTPUT :

Hello World!Welcome to Simple Java Programs

Program: Java Program Using "\n" in Print statement

```
//Using \n in print statement
public class Main
{
public static void main(String[] args)
{
System.out.print("Hello World!\n");
System.out.print("Welcome to Simple Java Programs");
}
}
```

OUTPUT :

Hello World!
Welcome to Simple Java Programs

Program: Java Program Using Only One Print statement

```
//Using only one print statement
public class Main
```

```
{
public static void main(String[] args)
{
System.out.print("Hello World!\nWelcome to Simple Java Programs");
}
}
```

OUTPUT :

```
Hello World!
Welcome to Simple Java Programs
```

Program: Java Program, Formatting with Print Statement

```
public class Main
{
public static void main(String[] args)
{
double value = 5.3697;
System.out.println(value);
System.out.printf("%.2f" , value);
}
}
```

OUTPUT :

```
5.3697
5.37
```

Program: Java Program, Formatting with Print Statement

```
class ChkPrint
{
public static void main(String[] args){
System.out.println("*\n**\n***\n****");
}
}
```

OUTPUT :

```
*
**
***
****
```

Program: Java Program, Formatting with Print Statement

```
class ChkPrint
```

```
{
public static void main(String[] args){
System.out.println("*****\n *** \n * \n *** \n*****");
}
}
```

OUTPUT :

```
****
***
*
***
*****
```

Program: Java Program, Formatting with Print Statement

```
class ChkPrint
{
public static void main(String[] args){
System.out.println(2+4+5);
}
}
```

OUTPUT :

```
11
```

Program: Java Program, Formatting with Print Statement

```
class ChkPrint
{
public static void main(String[] args)
{
System.out.println(45-32);
System.out.println(45*20);
}
}
```

OUTPUT :

```
13
900
```

Program: Java Program, Java Strings

```
class StrTestPgm
{
public static void main(String[] args)
```

```
{
char mychar = 'u';
System.out.println(mychar);
}
}
```

OUTPUT :

u

Program: Java Program to Assign and Print Values of Two Strings

```
class StrTestPgm
{
public static void main(String[] args)
{
String s1 = "String and Characters";
String s2 = new String("String and Characters Checking");
System.out.println(s1);
System.out.println(s2);
}
}
```

OUTPUT :

String and Characters Checking
String and Characters Checking

Program: Java Program Using Escape Sequence

```
class StrTestPgm
{
public static void main(String[] args)
{
String mystring = "This is \"Java\" programming course";
System.out.println(mystring);
}
}
```

OUTPUT :

This is "Java" programming course

Program: Java Program Using Java String Methods and Operations

//Java charAt()

```
class StrTestPgm
{
public static void main(String[] args)
{
String s1 = "Hello";
char ch = s1.charAt(0);
System.out.println(ch);
}
}
```

OUTPUT:

H

Program: Java Program Using Java String Methods and Operations

//Java length()

//It returns the length (number of characters) in a string.

```
class StrTestPgm
{
public static void main(String[] args)
{
String s1 = "Hello World";
int len = s1.length();
System.out.println("String length is " + len);
}
}
```

OUTPUT:

String length is 11

Program: Java Program Using Java String Methods and Operations

```
class StrTestPgm
{
public static void main(String[] args)
{
String s1 = "Umbrella";
String s2 = s1.substring(2);
String s3 = s1.substring(2, 6);
System.out.println(s2);
System.out.println(s3);
}
```

```
}
```

OUTPUT:

brella
brel

Program: Java Program Using Java String Methods and Operations

//Java isEmpty()

```
class StrTestPgm
{
public static void main(String[] args)
{
String s1 = "Umbrella";
String s2 = "";
System.out.println(s1.isEmpty());
System.out.println(s2.isEmpty());
}
}
```

OUTPUT:

false
true

Program: Java Program Using Java String Methods and Operations

//Java concat()

```
class StrTestPgm
{
public static void main(String[] args)
{
String s1 = "Java ";
String s2 = "Programming";
s1 = s1.concat(s2);
System.out.println(s1);
}
}
```

OUTPUT:

Java Programming

Program: Java Program Using Java String Methods and Operations

//Java replace()

```
class StrTestPgm
  {
  public static void main(String[] args)
  {
  String s1 = "Welcome to Java Programming";
  String s2 = s1.replace('o', 'D');
  System.out.println(s2);
  }
  }
```

OUTPUT:

WelcDme tD Java PrDgramming

Program: Java Program Using Java String Methods and Operations

```
class StrTestPgm
  {
  public static void main(String[] args)
  {
  String s1 = "Switch on the button";
  String s2 = s1.replace("on", "ON");
  System.out.println(s2);
  }
  }
```

OUTPUT:

Switch ON the buttON

Program: Java Program Using Java String Methods and Operations

```
class StrTestPgm
  {
  public static void main(String[] args)
  {
  String s1 = "Welcome to Java Programming";
  String s2 = s1.toLowerCase();
  System.out.println(s2);
  }
  }
```

OUTPUT:

welcome to java programming

Program: Java Program Using Java String Methods and Operations

//Java toUpperCase()

```
class StrTestPgm
    {
    public static void main(String[] args)
    {
    String s1 = "Welcome to Java Programming"
    String s2 = s1.toUpperCase();
    System.out.println(s2);
    }
    }
```

OUTPUT:

WELCOME TO JAVA PROGRAMMING

Program: Java Program Using Java String Methods and Operations

//Java indexOf()

```
class StrTestPgm
    {
    public static void main(String[] args)
    {
    String s1 = "Switch on the button";
    int n1 = s1.indexOf('t');
    int n2 = s1.indexOf("on");
    System.out.println("n1 = " + n1);
    System.out.println("n2 = " + n2);
    }
    }
```

OUTPUT:

n1 = 3
n2 = 7

Program: Java Program Using Java String Methods and Operations

//Java contains()

```
class StrTestPgm
   {
   public static void main(String[] args)
   {
   String s1 = "My name is : Robert Brown";
   System.out.println(s1.contains("Robe"));
   System.out.println(s1.contains(":"));
   System.out.println(s1.contains("/"));
   }
   }
```

OUTPUT:

```
true
true
false
```

Program: Java Program Using Java String Methods and Operations

//Java compareTo()

```
class StrTestPgm
   {
   public static void main(String[] args)
   {
   String s1 = "Black";
   String s2 = "Brown";
   System.out.println(s1.compareTo(s2));
   }
   }
```

OUTPUT:

```
-6
```

Program: Java Program Using Java String Methods and Operations

//Java String Operations

//Java Concatenation (+)

```
class StrTestPgm
   {
```

```
publicstaticvoid main(String[] args)
{
String s1 = "Codes";
String s2 = "Java";
String s3 = s1 + s2;
System.out.println(s3);
}
}
```

Output

CodesJava

Program: Java Program Using Java String Methods and Operations

//Java Comparison (==, !=)

```
class StrTestPgm
{
publicstaticvoid main(String[] args)
{
String s1 = "Black";
String s2 = "Black";
System.out.println(s1 == s2);
System.out.println(s1 != s2);
}
}
```

OUTPUT:

true
false

Program: Java Program Using Java String Methods and Operations

```
classStrTestPgm
{
publicstaticvoid main(String[] args)
{
String s1 = "Black";
String s2 = "black";
System.out.println(s1 == s2);
System.out.println(s1 != s2);
}
}
```

OUTPUT:

false
true

Program: Java Program Using Java String Methods and Operations

//Difference between equals() method and ==

```
class StrTestPgm
{
publicstaticvoid main(String[] args)
{
String s1 = new String("Welcome");
String s2 = new String("Welcome");
if (s1 == s2) System.out.println("Both objects are equal");
else System.out.println("Objects are different");
}
}
```

OUTPUT:

Objects are different

Program: Java Program Using Java String Methods and Operations

```
class StrTestPgm
{
publicstaticvoid main(String[] args)
{
String s1 = new String("Welcome");
String s2 = s1;
if (s1 == s2)
System.out.println("Both objects are equal");
else
System.out.println("Objects are different");
}
}
```

OUTPUT:

Both objects are equal

Program: Java Program Using Java String Methods and Operations

```
class StrTestPgm
{
publicstaticvoid main(String[] args)
{
String s1 = new String("Welcome");
String s2 = new String("Welcome");
if (s1.equals(s2))
```

```
System.out.println("Values of both objects are equal");
else
System.out.println("Values of both objects are not equal");
}
}
```

OUTPUT:

Values of both objects are equal

CHAPTER THREE

Data Types, Variables, Operators

Program: Java Program to store and display values

```
public class PrintPattern
    {
    public class Exercise_DataType_1
    {
    public static void main(String[] args)
    {
    int a = 10;
    double b = 20.3;
    double c = 3.14785;
    System.out.println("The value of a is : "+ a);
    System.out.println("The value of b is : "+ b);
    System.out.println("The value of c is : "+ c);
    }
    }
```

OUTPUT:

The value of a is : 10
The value of b is : 20.3
The value of c is : 3.14785

Program: Java Program using boolean datatype

```
package SimpleJavaPrograms;
    public class BooleanTestExercise
    {
    public static void main(String[] args)
    {
    //Use the boolean keyword to declare boolean variable
    boolean testResult;
    //Initialize the boolean variable with value true or false, once boolean declaration is done
    testResult = true;
    //Print the value of boolean variable
    System.out.println("Test Result is: " + testResult);
    //Change the value of boolean variable
```

```
testResult = false;
//Print the value of boolean variable
System.out.println("Test Result is: " + testResult);
}
}
```

OUTPUT :

Test Result is: true
Test Result is: false

Program: Java Program using boolean datatype

```
public class Exercise_DataType_2
{
public static void main(String[] args)
{
boolean value = true;
value = false;
System.out.println("The value for the Boolean variable is : "+ value);
}
}
```

OUTPUT:

The value for the Boolean variable is : false

Program: Java Program using integer datatype

```
package SimpleJavaPrograms;
public class IntegerTestExersice
{
public static void main(String[] args)
{
//Use the int keyword to declare integer variable
int carSpeed;
//Initialize the integer variable with value 20
carSpeed = 20;
//Print the value of integer variable
System.out.println("Car is running at the speed of: " + carSpeed);
//Change the value of integer variable
carSpeed = carSpeed + 20;
//Print the value of integer variable
System.out.println("Current speed of the car is: " + carSpeed);
}
}
```

OUTPUT :

Car is running at the speed of : 20
Current speed of the car is: 40

Program: Java Program using char datatype

```
package SimpleJavaPrograms;
    public class CharTestExercise
    {
    public static void main(String[] args)
    {
    //Use the char keyword to declare character variable
    char a;
    //Initialize the char variable with value 'P'
    a = 'P';
    //Print the value of char variable
    System.out.println("Value of char is : " + a);
    }
    }
```

OUTPUT :

Value of char is : P

Program: Java Program using double datatype

```
package SimpleJavaPrograms;
    public class DoubleTestExercise
    {
    public static void main(String[] args)
    {
    //Use the double keyword to declare decimal variable
    double PI;
    //Initialize the double variable with value 'P'
    PI = 3.14159;
    //Print the value of double variable
    System.out.print("PI: " + PI);
    }
    }
```

OUTPUT :

PI: 3.14159

Program: Java Program using Assignment Operators

```
public class Assignment_Operators
```

```
{
//Normal Assignment
static int speed = 80; // speed variable gets the data 80
static int distance = 20; // distance variable gets the data 20
static int time = 10; // time variable gets the data 10
static String name = "ToolsQA"; // name variable gets the data ToolsQA
static boolean isGood = true; // isGood variable gets the data true
public static void main(String[] args)
{
System.out.println("Data stored in the speed variable is : " + speed);
System.out.println("Data stored in the distance variable is : " + distance);
System.out.println("Data stored in the time variable is : " + time);
System.out.println("Data stored in the name variable is : " + name);
System.out.println("Data stored in the isGood variable is : " + isGood);
speed = 100; // Previous data of speed is overwritten with 100
time = distance; // Previous data of time is overwritten with distance data
name = "ForumsQA"; // Previous data of name is overwritten with ForumsQA
isGood = false; // Previous data of isGood is overwritten with false
System.out.println("Data stored in the speed variable is : " + speed);
System.out.println("Data stored in the time variable is : " + time);
System.out.println("Data stored in the name variable is : " + name);
System.out.println("Data stored in the isGood variable is : " + isGood);
//Multiple Assignments
speed = distance = 0; // 100 (20 = 0)
System.out.println("Data stored in the speed variable is : " + speed);
//Illegal Assignments - Compile time errors
speed = "ToolsQA"; //String can not be assign to integer
name = 10; // Integer can not be assign to String
isGood = "ToolsQa" // String can not be assign to Boolean
}
}
```

OUTPUT :

Data stored in the speed variable is : 80
Data stored in the distance variable is : 20
Data stored in the time variable is : 10
Data stored in the name variable is : ToolsQA
Data stored in the isGood variable is : true
Data stored in the speed variable is : 100
Data stored in the time variable is : 20
Data stored in the name variable is : ForumsQA
Data stored in the isGood variable is : false
Data stored in the speed variable is : 0

Program: Java Program using Arithmetic Operators

```
package SimpleJavaPrograms;
```

```
public class Arithmetic_Operators
{
public static void main(String[] args)
{
int a, b = 10, c = 5;
a = b + c;
System.out.println("Data stored in ‘a’ after ‘+’ Arithmetic operation is " + a);
a = b - c;
System.out.println("Data stored in ‘a’ after ‘-’ Arithmetic operation is " + a);
a = b * c;
System.out.println("Data stored in ‘a’ after ‘*’ Arithmetic operation is " + a);
a = b / c;
System.out.println("Data stored in ‘a’ after ‘/’ Arithmetic operation is " + a);
a = b % c;
System.out.println("Data stored in ‘a’ after ‘%’ Arithmetic operation is " + a);
b++;
System.out.println("Data stored in ‘b’ after ‘++’ Arithmetic operation is " + b);
c--;
System.out.println("Data stored in ‘c’ after ‘--’ Arithmetic operation is " + c);
}
}
```

OUTPUT :

Data stored in ‘a’ after ‘+’ Arithmetic operation is 15
Data stored in ‘a’ after ‘-’ Arithmetic operation is 5
Data stored in ‘a’ after ‘’ Arithmetic operation is 50*
Data stored in ‘a’ after ‘/’ Arithmetic operation is 2
Data stored in ‘a’ after ‘%’ Arithmetic operation is 0
Data stored in ‘b’ after ‘++’ Arithmetic operation is 11
Data stored in ‘c’ after ‘--’ Arithmetic operation is 4

Program: Java Program using Relational Operators

```
package SimpleJavaPrograms;
public class Relational_Operators
{
public static void main(String[] args)
{
int One = 1;
int Two = 2;
int Three = 3;
System.out.println("<<<<<< GREATER THAN OPERATOR >>>>>>");
System.out.println(" One > Two ==> " + (One > Two)); //false
System.out.println(" Two > One ==> " + (Two > One)); //true
System.out.println(" Three > Two ==> " + (Three > Two)); //true
System.out.println("<<<<<< GREATER THAN OR EQUAL TO OPERATOR >>>>>>");
System.out.println(" One >= Two ==> " + (One >= Two)); //false
```

```
System.out.println(" Two >= One ==> " + (Two >= One)); //true
System.out.println(" Three >= Two ==> " + (Three >= Two)); //true
System.out.println("<<<<<< LESS THAN OPERATOR >>>>>>");
System.out.println(" One < Two ==> " + (One < Two)); //true
System.out.println(" Two < One ==> " + (Two < One)); //false
System.out.println(" Three < Two ==> " + (Three < Two)); //false
//less than or equal to
System.out.println("<<<<<< LESS THAN OR EQUAL TO OPERATOR >>>>>>");
System.out.println(" One <= Two ==> " + (One <= Two)); //true
System.out.println(" Two <= One ==> " + (Two <= One)); //false
System.out.println(" Three <= Two ==> " + (Three <= Two)); //false
//equal to
System.out.println("<<<<<< EQUAL TO OPERATOR >>>>>>");
System.out.println(" One == Two ==> " + (One == Two)); //false
System.out.println(" Three == Two + One ==> " + (Three == Two+One)); //true
//not equal to
System.out.println("<<<<<< NOT EQUAL TO OPERATOR >>>>>>");
System.out.println(" One != Two ==> " + (One != Two)); //true
System.out.println(" Three != Two + One ==> " + (Three != Two + One)); //false
}
}
```

OUTPUT :

```
<<<<<< GREATER THAN OPERATOR >>>>>
 One > Two ==> false
 Two > One ==> true
 Three > Two ==> true
 <<<<<< GREATER THAN OR EQUAL TO OPERATOR >>>>>>
 One >= Two ==> false
 Two >= One ==> true
 Three >= Two ==> true
 <<<<<< LESS THAN OPERATOR >>>>>>
 One < Two ==> true
 Two < One ==> false
 Three < Two ==> false
 <<<<<< LESS THAN OR EQUAL TO OPERATOR >>>>>>
 One <= Two ==> true
 Two <= One ==> false
 Three <= Two ==> false
 <<<<<< EQUAL TO OPERATOR >>>>>>
 One == Two ==> false
 Three == Two + One ==> true <<<<<< NOT EQUAL TO OPERATOR >>>>>>
 One != Two ==> true
 Three != Two + One ==> false
```

Program: Java Program using Logical Operators

```
package SimpleJavaPrograms;
public class Logical_Operators
{
public static void main(String[] args)
{
boolean Output_1 = true;
boolean Output_2 = false;
System.out.println("Check if both the boolean variables are true : " + (Output_1 && Output_2));
System.out.println("Check if even one of the boolean varibale is true : " + (Output_1 || Output_2));
System.out.println("Change the state of the Output_1 to false : " + (!Output_1));
}
}
```

OUTPUT :

Check if both the boolean variables are true : false
Check if even one of the boolean variable is true : true
Change the state of the Output_1 to false : false

Program: Java Program using Conditional Operators

```
package SimpleJavaPrograms;
public class Conditional_Operators
{
public static void main(String[] args)
{
int Ten = 10;
int Twenty = 20;
int Thirty = 30;
boolean bData;
int iData;
bData = (Thirty == Twenty + Ten) ? true: false;
System.out.println( "The boolean data of the variable 'bData' is : " + bData ); //true
iData = ((Thirty == Twenty + Ten)) ? 50: 100;
System.out.println( "The int Data of the variable iData is : " + iData ); //50
//This is a use of Not Logical Operator
iData = (!(Thirty == Twenty + Ten)) ? 50: 100;
System.out.println( "The int Data of the variable iData is : " + iData ); //100
}
}
```

OUTPUT :

The boolean data of the variable 'bData' is : true
The int Data of the variable iData is : 50
The int Data of the variable iData is : 100

Program: Java Program, Encapsulation

```
class Student
{
// private variable
private String name;
// public method
publicvoid setName(String n)
{
name = n;
}
// public method
public String getName()
{
return name;
}
}
class Test
{
publicstaticvoid main(String[] args)
{
Student st = new Student();
// accessing public method
st.setName("JohnSmith");
// accessing public method
System.out.println(st.getName());
}
}
```

OUTPUT:

JohnSmith

Program: Java Program Using static Keyword

```
class Student
{
String name;
public Student(String n)
{
name = n;
}
}
class Test
{
publicstaticvoid main(String[] args)
{
Student st1 = new Student("JohnSmith");
Student st2 = new Student("JulieThomas");
System.out.println(st1.name);
```

```
System.out.println(st2.name);
}
}
```

OUTPUT:

JohnSmith
JulieThomas

Program: Java Program Using static Variables

```
class Student
{
String name;
String college = "xyz";
public Student(String n)
{
name = n;
}
}
class Test
{
publicstaticvoid main(String[] args)
{
Student st1 = new Student("John");
Student st2 = new Student("Julie");
System.out.println("Name: " + st1.name);
System.out.println("College: " + st1.college);
System.out.println("Name: " + st2.name);
System.out.println("College: " + st2.college);
}
}
```

OUTPUT:

Name: John
College: xyz
Name: Julie
College: xyz

Program: Java Program Using static Keyword

```
class Student
{
String name;
static String college = "XYZ";
public Student(String n)
{
```

```
name = n;
}
}
class Test
{
publicstaticvoid main(String[] args)
{
Student st1 = new Student("John");
Student st2 = new Student("Julie");
System.out.println("Name: " + st1.name);
System.out.println("College: " + st1.college);
System.out.println("Name: " + st2.name);
System.out.println("College: " + st2.college);
}
}
```

Output

Name: John
College: XYZ
Name: Julie
College: XYZ

Program: Java Program Using static Keyword

```
class Student
{
static String college = "IIT";
}
class Test
{
publicstaticvoid main(String[] args)
{
System.out.println("College Name: " + Student.college);
}
}
```

OUTPUT:

College Name:

IIT

Program: Simple Java Program

```
Program of class Counter
{
int count = 0;
Counter()
```

```
{
count++;
System.out.println("Object: " + count);
}
}
class Test
{
publicstaticvoid main(String[] args)
{
Counter c1 = new Counter();
Counter c2 = new Counter();
Counter c3 = new Counter();
Counter c4 = new Counter();
}
}
```

OUTPUT:

Object: 1
Object: 1
Object: 1
Object: 1

Program: Java Program Using static Keyword

```
class Counter
{
staticint count = 0;
Counter()
{
count++;
System.out.println("No of objects: " + count);
}
}
class Test
{
publicstaticvoid main(String[] args)
{
Counter c1 = new Counter();
Counter c2 = new Counter();
Counter c3 = new Counter();
Counter c4 = new Counter();
}
}
```

Output

No of objects: 1
No of objects: 2
No of objects: 3

No of objects: 4

Program: Java Program Using static Method

```
class Student
{
// non-static variable
String name;
// static variable
static String college = "IIT";
public Student(String n)
{
name = n;
}
// static method
publicstaticvoid updateCollege()
{
college = "NIT";
}
// non-static method
publicvoid printDetails()
{
System.out.println("Name: " + name + ", College: " + college);
}
}
class Test
{
publicstaticvoid main(String[] args)
{
Student st1 = new Student("John");
Student st2 = new Student("Julie");
// calling static method
Student.updateCollege();
st1.printDetails();
st2.printDetails();
}
}
```

Output

Name: John, College: NIT
Name: Julie, College: NIT

Program: Java Program Using static Block

```
class Test
{
publicstaticvoid main(String[] args)
{
System.out.println("This is a random statement");
```

```
// block
{
int num = 10;
num++;
System.out.println(num);
}
}
}
```

OUTPUT:

This is a random statement
11

CHAPTER FOUR

Control Flow

Decision-Making Statements

Program: Java Program for IF Statements

```
class IfStatement {
public static void main(String args[]) {
int A = 15 ;
if ( A < 35 ) {
System.out.println("Statement 'if' is true") ;}
}
}
```

OUTPUT:

Statement 'if' is true

Program: Java Program Using IF ELSE statements

```
class IfElseStatement {
public static void main(String args[]) {
int A = 40 ;
if ( A >= 30 ) {
System.out.println("Statement 'if' is true") ;} else {
System.out.println("Statement 'else' is true");}
}
}
```

OUTPUT:

Statement 'else' is true

Program: Java Program to find even or odd number

```
class EvenOddProgram
   {
   public static void main(String [] args)
```

```
{
int num1 = 22;
if(num1 % 2 == 0)
{
System.out.println(num1+ " is an even number");
}
else
{
System.out.println(num1+ " is an odd number");
}
}
}
Output :
22 is an even number
```

Program: Java Program Using IF THEN statements

```
package SimpleJavaPrograms;
    public class IfThen_Statement
    {
    public static void main(String[] args)
    {
    String sDay = "Friday";
    int iDay = 5;
    if(sDay.equals("Friday")){
    System.out.println("Today is Friday");
    }
    if(iDay==7){
    System.out.println("Today is Friday");
    }
    }
    }
```

OUTPUT:

Today is Friday
Today is Friday

Program: Java Program Using IF THEN ELSE statements

```
package SimpleJavaPrograms;
    public class IfThenElse_Statement
    {
    public static void main(String[] args)
    {
    String sDay = "Saturday";
    int iDay = 6;
    if(sDay.equals("Tuesday")){
```

```
System.out.println("Today is Tuesday");
}
else
{
System.out.println("Today is not Tuesday");
}
if(iDay==7){
System.out.println("Today is Tuesday");
}
else
{
System.out.println("Today is not Tuesday");
}
}
}
```

OUTPUT:

Today is not Tuesday
Today is not Tuesday

Program: Java Program Using IF ELSE IF statements

```
class IfElseStatement
{
public static void main(String args[])
{
int A = 30 ;
if ( A < 20 )
{
System.out.println("Statement 'if' is true") ;
}
else if ( A==30 )
{
System.out.println("Statement 'else if' is true");
}
else
{
System.out.println("Statement 'else' is true");
}

}

}
```

OUTPUT:

Statement ‘else if’ is true

Program : Java Program Using Nested if Statement

```
class NestedIfStatement
    {
public static void main(String args[])
    {
int A = 50 ;
    int B = 60 ;
if ( A == 50 )
    {
System.out.println(" 'if' Statement1 is true and A = 50 ") ;
    if ( B == 60 )
    {
System.out.println(" 'if' Statement2 is true and B = 60 ");
    }
}
}
}
```

OUTPUT:

'if' Statement1 is true and A = 50
'if' Statement2 is true and B = 60

Program: Java Program Using IF THEN ELSE IF statements

```
package SimpleJavaPrograms;
    public class IfThenElseIf_Statement
    {
    public static void main(String[] args)
    {
    String sDay = "Monday";
    int iDay = 1;
    if(sDay.equals("Sunday")){
    System.out.println("Today is Sunday");
    }else if(sDay.equals("Saturday")){
    System.out.println("Today is not Saturday");
    }
    else
    {
    System.out.println("Today is a Weekday");
    }
    if(iDay==7)
    {
    System.out.println("Today is Sunday");
    }
    else if(iDay==6)
    {
```

```
System.out.println("Today is Saturday");
}
else
{
System.out.println("Today is a Weekday");
}
}
}
```

OUTPUT:

Today is a Weekday
Today is a Weekday

Program: Program to find greatest of three numbers

```
class GreatestOfThreeNumber
{
public static void main(String [] args)
{
int num1 = 30, num2 = 10, num3 = 40;
if(num1 > num2)
{
if(num1 > num3)
System.out.println("Greatest number = "+num1);
else
System.out.println("Greatest number = "+num3);
}
else
{
if(num2 > num3)
System.out.println("Greatest number = "+num2);
else
System.out.println("Greatest number = "+num3);
}
}
}
```

OUTPUT:

Greatest number = 40

Program: Program to find greatest of three numbers

OUTPUT:

A grade

Program: Java Program Using Switch statement

```
package SimpleJavaPrograms;
    public class Switch_Statement
    {
    public static void main(String[] args)
    {
    int iDa
    class FindingGrade
    {
    public static void main(String [] args)
    {
    int marks = 65;
    if(marks >= 80)
    System.out.println("A+ grade");
    else if(marks >= 60 && marks < 80)
    System.out.println("A grade");
    else if(marks >= 40 && marks < 60)
    System.out.println("B grade");
    else if(marks >= 30 && marks < 40)
    System.out.println("C grade");
    else
    System.out.println("D grade");
    }
    }
    y = 1;
    String sDay = "Wednesday";
    switch(iDay)
    {
    case 1:
    System.out.println("Today is Monday");
    break;
    case 3:
    System.out.println("Today is Tuesday");
    break;
    case 4:
    System.out.println("Today is Wednesday");
    break;
    case 5:
    System.out.println("Today is Thursday");
    break;
    case 6:
    System.out.println("Today is Friday");
    break;
    case 7:
    System.out.println("Today is Saturday");
    break;
```

```
default:
System.out.println("Today is Sunday");
break;
}
switch(sDay){
case "Monday":
System.out.println("Today is Monday");
break;
case "Tuesday":
System.out.println("Today is Tuesday");
break;
case "Wednesday":
System.out.println("Today is Wednesday");
break;
case "Thursday":
System.out.println("Today is Thursday");
break;
case "Friday":
System.out.println("Today is Friday");
break;
case "Saturday":
System.out.println("Today is Saturday");
break;
default:
System.out.println("Today is Sunday");
break;
}
}
}
```

OUTPUT:

Today is Wednesday
Today is Wednesday

Program: Java Program For Finding 'a' And 'b' Using Nested Switch

```
import java.util.Scanner;
public class example {
public static void main(String[] args) {
int a,b;
System.out.println("Enter a and b");
Scanner in = new Scanner(System.in);
a = in.nextInt();
b = in.nextInt();
// Outer Switch starts here
switch (a) {
// If a = 1
```

```
case 1:
// Inner Switch starts here
switch (b) {
// for condition b = 1
case 1:
System.out.println("b is 1");
break;
// for condition b = 2
case 2:
System.out.println("b is 2");
break;
// for condition b = 3
case 3:
System.out.println("b is 3");
break;
}
break;
// for condition a = 2
case 2:
System.out.println("a is 2");
break;
// for condition a == 3
case 3:
System.out.println("a is 3");
break;
default:
System.out.println("default statement here");
break;
}
}
}
```

OUTPUT:

```
Enter a and b
1
3
B is 3
```

Program: Java Program Switch Statement Using String

```
import java.util.Scanner;
public class example
{
public static void main(String[] args)
{
String mobile = "iPhone";
switch (mobile) {
```

```
case "samsung":
System.out.println("Buy a Samsung phone");
break;
case "iPhone":
System.out.println("Buy an XIAOMI");
break;
case "Motorola":
System.out.println("Buy a Motorola phone");
}
}
}
```

OUTPUT:

Buy an XIAOMI

Program: Java Program using Wrapper In A Switch Statement

```
public class example
{
public static void main(String[] args)
{
// Initializing a Wrapper variable
Integer x = 3;
// Switch statement with Wrapper variable x
switch (x)
{
case 1:
System.out.println("Value of x = 1");
break;
case 2:
System.out.println("Value of x = 2");
break;
case 3:
System.out.println("Value of x = 3");
break;
// Default case statement
default:
System.out.println("Value of x is undefined");
}
}
}
```

OUTPUT:

value of x=3

Program: Java Program Using Branching / Loop Control Statements

```
class BreakStatement
    {
public static void main(String args[])
    {
for(int a = 8 ; a < 12 ; a++)
    {
if ( a == 10 )
    {
    break ;
    }
System.out.println("Value of a =" + a) ;
    }
    }
    }
```

OUTPUT:

```
Value of a = 8
Value of a = 9
```

Program: Java Program Using Continue Statement

Example:

```
    class ContinueStatement {
public static void main(String args[]) {
for(int x = 10 ; x <= 14 ; x++) {
if ( x == 12 ) {
continue ;
}
System.out.println("Value of x =" + x) ;
}
}
}
```

OUTPUT:

```
Value of x =10
Value of x =11
Value of x =13
Value of x =14
```

CHAPTER FIVE

Arrays

Program: Java Program Using Arrays

```
package SimpleJavaPrograms;
public class Array
{
public static void main(String[] args)
{
String [] aMake = {"SAMSUNG","NOKIA","REDMI","OPPO","APPLE"};
//This is to store the size of the Array
int iLength = aMake.length;
System.out.println("Length of the Array is ==> " + iLength);
//This is to access the first element of an array directly with it's position
String sSAMSUNG = aMake[0];
System.out.println("First data of the Array is ==> " + sSAMSUNG);
//This is to access the last element of an Array
String sAPPLE = aMake[iLength-1];
System.out.println("Last data of the Array is ==> " + sAPPLE);
//This is to print all the element datas of an Array
for(int i = 0;i<=iLength-1;i++){
System.out.println("The data stored at position "+i+" in aMake array is ==> " + aMake[i]);
}
}
}
```

OUTPUT:

Length of the Array is ==> 5
First data of the Array is ==> SAMSUNG
Last data of the Array is ==> APPLE
The data stored at position 0 in aMake array is ==> SAMSUNG
The data stored at position 1 in aMake array is ==> NOKIA
The data stored at position 2 in aMake array is ==> REDMI
The data stored at position 3 in aMake array is ==> OPPO
The data stored at position 4 in aMake array is ==> APPLE

Program: Java Program to Access Elements of an Array

```
class Main
    {
public static void main(String[] args)
    {
// create an array
int[] age = {12, 4, 5, 2, 5};
    // access each array elements
System.out.println("Accessing Elements of Array:");
System.out.println("First Element: " + age[0]);
System.out.println("Second Element: " + age[1]);
System.out.println("Third Element: " + age[2]);
System.out.println("Fourth Element: " + age[3]);
System.out.println("Fifth Element: " + age[4]);
}
}
```

OUTPUT:

```
Accessing Elements of Array:
    First Element: 12
    Second Element: 4
    Third Element: 5
    Fourth Element: 2
    Fifth Element: 5
```

Program: Java Program for Looping Through Array Elements

```
class Main {
public static void main(String[] args) {

// create an array
int[] age = {12, 4, 5};
    // loop through the array
// using for loop
System.out.println("Using for Loop:");
for(int i = 0; i < age.length; i++) {
System.out.println(age[i]);
}
}
}
```

OUTPUT:

```
Using for Loop:
    12
    4
    5
```

Program: Java Program to Pass an Array to a Method

```
package SimpleJavaPrograms;
    public class Passing_Array
    {
    public static void main(String[] args)
    {
    //Declaring an Array
    String [] aMake = {"SAMSUNG","NOKIA","REDMI","OPPO","APPLE"};
    // Calling Print Array method and passing an Array as a parameter
    Print_Array(aMake);
    }
    //This accept Array as an argument of type String
    public static void Print_Array(String []array){
    for(int i = 0;i<=array.length-1;i++){
    System.out.println("Printing all the datas of an Array ==> " + array[i]);
    }
    }
    }
```

OUTPUT:

Printing all the datas of an Array ==> SAMSUNG
Printing all the datas of an Array ==> NOKIA
Printing all the datas of an Array ==> REDMI
Printing all the datas of an Array ==> OPPO
Printing all the datas of an Array ==> APPLE

Program: Java Program Using the for-each Loop

```
class Main {
public static void main(String[] args) {

// create an array
int[] age = {12, 4, 5};
    // loop through the array
// using for loop
System.out.println("Using for-each Loop:");
for(int a : age) {
System.out.println(a);
}
}
}
```

OUTPUT:

Using for-each Loop:
12

4
5

Program: Java Program to Return an Array from a Method

```
package SimpleJavaPrograms;
public class Returning_Array
{
public static void main(String[] args)
{
String[] aMake = ReturnArray();
for(int i = 0;i<=aMake.length-1;i++){
System.out.println("Printing all the datas of an Array ==> " + aMake[i]);
}
}
//This method returns an Array of type String
public static String[] ReturnArray() {
String [] aArray = {"SAMSUNG","NOKIA","REDMI","OPPO","APPLE"};
return aArray;
}
}
```

OUTPUT:

Printing all the datas of an Array ==> SAMSUNG
Printing all the datas of an Array ==> NOKIA
Printing all the datas of an Array ==> REDMI
Printing all the datas of an Array ==> OPPO
Printing all the datas of an Array ==> APPLE

Program: Java Program to Append All Elements of Other Collection to Java ArrayList

```
import java.util.ArrayList;
import java.util.Vector;
public class AppendAllElementsOfOtherCollectionToArrayListExample {
public static void main(String[] args) {
//create an ArrayList object
ArrayList arrayList = new ArrayList();
//Add elements to Arraylist
arrayList.add("1");
arrayList.add("2");
arrayList.add("3");
//create a new Vector object
Vector v = new Vector();
v.add("4");
v.add("5");
/* To append all elements of another Collection to ArrayList use
boolean addAll(Collection c) method.
```

```
It returns true if the ArrayList was changed by the method call. */
//append all elements of Vector to ArrayList
arrayList.addAll(v);
//display elements of ArrayList
System.out.println("After appending all elements of Vector, ArrayList contains..");
for(int i=0; i<arrayList.size(); i++)
System.out.println(arrayList.get(i));
}
}
```

OUTPUT:

```
After appending all elements of Vector, ArrayList contains..
1
2
3
4
5
```

Program: Java Program to Copy all elements of Java ArrayList to an Object Array

```
import java.util.ArrayList;
public class CopyElementsOfArrayListToArrayExample {
public static void main(String[] args) {
//create an ArrayList object
ArrayList arrayList = new ArrayList();
//Add elements to ArrayList
arrayList.add("1");
arrayList.add("2");
arrayList.add("3");
arrayList.add("4");
arrayList.add("5");
/* To copy all elements of java ArrayList object into array use Object[] toArray() method. */
Object[] objArray = arrayList.toArray();
//display contents of Object array
System.out.println("ArrayList elements are copied into an Array. Now Array Contains..");
for(int index=0; index < objArray.length ; index++)
System.out.println(objArray[index]);
}
}
```

OUTPUT:

```
ArrayList elements are copied into an Array. Now Array Contains..
1
2
3
4
```

5

Program: Java Program to Get Size of Java ArrayList and loop through elements Example

```
import java.util.ArrayList;
    public class GetSizeOfArrayListExample
    {
    public static void main(String[] args)
    {
    //create an ArrayList object
    ArrayList arrayList = new ArrayList();
    //Add elements to Arraylist using
    arrayList.add("1");
    arrayList.add("2");
    arrayList.add("3");
    //To get size of Java ArrayList use int size() method
    int totalElements = arrayList.size();
    System.out.println("ArrayList contains...");
    //loop through it
    for(int index=0; index < totalElements; index++)
    System.out.println(arrayList.get(index));
    }
    }
```

OUTPUT:

```
ArrayList contains...
    1
    2
    3
```

Program: Java Program to Get Sub List of Java ArrayList

```
import java.util.ArrayList;
    import java.util.List;
    public class GetSubListOfJavaArrayListExample
    {
    public static void main(String[] args)
    {
    //create an ArrayList object
    ArrayList arrayList = new ArrayList();
    //Add elements to Arraylist
    arrayList.add("1");
    arrayList.add("2");
    arrayList.add("3");
    arrayList.add("4");
    arrayList.add("5");
    /* To get a sub list of Java ArrayList use List subList(int startIndex, int endIndex) method.
```

```
This method returns an object of type List containing elements from startIndex to endIndex - 1.
*/
List lst = arrayList.subList(1,3);
//display elements of sub list.
System.out.println("Sub list contains : ");
for(int i=0; i< lst.size() ; i++)
System.out.println(lst.get(i));
/* Sub List returned by subList method is backed by original Arraylist. So any changes made to sub list will also
be REFLECTED in the original Arraylist. */
//remove one element from sub list
Object obj = lst.remove(0);
System.out.println(obj + " is removed from sub list");
//print original ArrayList
System.out.println("After removing " + obj + " from sub list, original ArrayList contains : ");
for(int i=0; i< arrayList.size() ; i++)
System.out.println(arrayList.get(i));
}
}
```

OUTPUT:

```
Sub list contains :
2
3
2 is removed from sub list
After removing 2 from sub list original ArrayList contains :
1
3
4
5
```

Program: Java Program to Iterate Through Elements Java ArrayList using Iterator

```
import java.util.ArrayList;
import java.util.Iterator;
public class IterateThroughArrayListUsingIteratorExample {
public static void main(String[] args) {
//create an ArrayList object
ArrayList arrayList = new ArrayList();
//Add elements to Arraylist
arrayList.add("1");
arrayList.add("2");
arrayList.add("3");
arrayList.add("4");
arrayList.add("5");
//get an Iterator object for ArrayList using iterator() method.
Iterator itr = arrayList.iterator();
//use hasNext() and next() methods of Iterator to iterate through the elements
```

```
System.out.println("Iterating through ArrayList elements...");
while(itr.hasNext())
System.out.println(itr.next());
}
}
```

OUTPUT:

Iterating through ArrayList elements...
1
2
3
4
5

Program: Java Program Remove All Elements From Java ArrayList

```
import java.util.ArrayList;
public class RemoveAllElementsOfArrayListExample {
public static void main(String[] args) {
//create an ArrayList object
ArrayList arrayList = new ArrayList();
//Add elements to Arraylist
arrayList.add("1");
arrayList.add("2");
arrayList.add("3");
System.out.println("Size of ArrayList before removing elements : "+ arrayList.size());
/* To remove all elements from the ArrayList use void clear() method. */
arrayList.clear();
System.out.println("Size of ArrayList after removing elements : " + arrayList.size());
}
}
```

OUPUT:

Size of ArrayList before removing elements : 3
Size of ArrayList after removing elements : 0

Program: Java Program to Remove An Element From Specified Index of Java ArrayList

```
import java.util.ArrayList;
public class RemoveElementFromArrayListExample
{
public static void main(String[] args) {
//create an ArrayList object
ArrayList arrayList = new ArrayList();
//Add elements to Arraylist
arrayList.add("1");
```

```
arrayList.add("2");
arrayList.add("3");
/* To remove an element from the specified index of ArrayList use Object remove(int index) method.
It returns the element that was removed from the ArrayList. */
Object obj = arrayList.remove(1);
System.out.println(obj + " is removed from ArrayList");
System.out.println("ArrayList contains...");
//display elements of ArrayList
for(int index=0; index < arrayList.size(); index++)
System.out.println(arrayList.get(index));
}
}
```

OUPUT:

```
2 is removed from ArrayList
ArrayList contains...
1
3
```

Program: Java Program to Replace an Element At Specified Index of Java ArrayList

```
import java.util.ArrayList;
public class ReplaceElementAtSpecifiedIndexArrayListExample
{
public static void main(String[] args)
{
//create an ArrayList object
ArrayList arrayList = new ArrayList();
//Add elements to Arraylist
arrayList.add("1");
arrayList.add("2");
arrayList.add("3");
/* To replace an element at the specified index of ArrayList use Object set(int index, Object obj) method. This
method replaces the specified element at the specified index in the ArrayList and returns the element previously at
the specified position. */
arrayList.set(1,"REPLACED ELEMENT");
System.out.println("ArrayList contains...");
//display elements of ArrayList
for(int index=0; index < arrayList.size(); index++)
System.out.println(arrayList.get(index));
}
}
```

OUTPUT:

```
ArrayList contains...
1
```

REPLACED ELEMENT
3

Program: Java Program To Search An Element Of Java ArrayList

```
import java.util.ArrayList;
public class SearchAnElementInArrayListExample {
public static void main(String[] args) {
//create an ArrayList object
ArrayList arrayList = new ArrayList();
//Add elements to Arraylist
arrayList.add("1");
arrayList.add("2");
arrayList.add("3");
arrayList.add("4");
arrayList.add("5");
arrayList.add("1");
arrayList.add("2");
/* To check whether the specified element exists in Java ArrayList use boolean contains(Object element) method.
It returns true if the ArrayList contains the specified objct, false otherwise. */
boolean blnFound = arrayList.contains("2");
System.out.println("Does arrayList contain 2 ? " + blnFound);
/* To get an index of specified element in ArrayList use int indexOf(Object element) method.
This method returns the index of the specified element in ArrayList. It returns -1 if not found. */
int index = arrayList.indexOf("4");
if(index == -1)
System.out.println("ArrayList does not contain 4");
else
System.out.println("ArrayList contains 4 at index :" + index);
/* To get last index of specified element in ArrayList use int lastIndexOf(Object element) method. This method
returns index of the last occurrence of the specified element in ArrayList. It returns -1 if not found. */
int lastIndex = arrayList.lastIndexOf("1");
if(lastIndex == -1)
System.out.println("ArrayList does not contain 1");
else
System.out.println("Last occurrence of 1 in ArrayList is at index :" + lastIndex);
}
}
```

OUTPUT:

```
Does arrayList contain 2 ? true
ArrayList contains 4 at index :3
Last occurrence of 1 in ArrayList is at index :5
```

Program: Java Program for ArrayList

```
import java.util.ArrayList;
```

```
public class SimpleArrayListExample {
public static void main(String[] args) {
//create an ArrayList object
ArrayList arrayList = new ArrayList();
/* Add elements to Arraylist using boolean add(Object o) method. It returns true as a general behavior of Collection.add method. The specified object is appended at the end of the ArrayList. */
arrayList.add("1");
arrayList.add("2");
arrayList.add("3");
/* Use get method of Java ArrayList class to display elements of ArrayList. Object get(int index) returns and element at the specified index in the ArrayList */
System.out.println("Getting elements of ArrayList");
System.out.println(arrayList.get(0));
System.out.println(arrayList.get(1));
System.out.println(arrayList.get(2));
}
}
```

OUTPUT:

```
Getting elements of ArrayList
1
2
3
```

Program: Java Program To Sort Elements of ArrayList

```
import java.util.ArrayList;
import java.util.Collections;
public class SortJavaArrayListExample {
public static void main(String[] args) {
//create an ArrayList object
ArrayList arrayList = new ArrayList();
//Add elements to Arraylist
arrayList.add("1");
arrayList.add("3");
arrayList.add("5");
arrayList.add("2");
arrayList.add("4");
/* To sort an ArrayList object, use Collection.sort method. This is a static method. It sorts an arrayList object's elements into ascending order. */
Collections.sort(arrayList);
//display elements of ArrayList
System.out.println("ArrayList elements after sorting in ascending order : ");
for(int i=0; i<arrayList.size(); i++)
System.out.println(arrayList.get(i));
}
}
```

OUTPUT:

```
ArrayList elements after sorting in ascending order :
    1
    2
    3
    4
    5
```

Program: Java Program to Add an element to specified index of Java ArrayList

```
import java.util.ArrayList;
    public class AddElementToSpecifiedIndexArrayListExample {
    public static void main(String[] args) {
    //create an ArrayList object
    ArrayList arrayList = new ArrayList();
    //Add elements to Arraylist
    arrayList.add("1");
    arrayList.add("2");
    arrayList.add("3");
    /* To add an element at the specified index of ArrayList use void add(int index, Object obj) method. This method
inserts the specified element at the specified index in the ArrayList. */
    arrayList.add(1,"INSERTED ELEMENT");
    /* Please note that add method DOES NOT overwrites the element previously at the specified index in the list. It
shifts the elements to right side and increasing the list size by 1. */
    System.out.println("ArrayList contains...");
    //display elements of ArrayList
    for(int index=0; index < arrayList.size(); index++)
    System.out.println(arrayList.get(index));
    }
    }
```

OUTPUT:

```
ArrayList contains...
    1
    INSERTED ELEMENT
    2
    3
```

CHAPTER SIX

Classes, Inheritance – Super classes- sub classes –Protected members

Program: Java Program using Classes

```
/* A program that uses the Box class*/
class Box
{
double width;
double height;
double depth;
}
// This class declares an object of type Box.
class BoxDemo
{
public static void main(String args[])
{
Box mybox = new Box();
double vol;
// assign values to mybox's instance variables
mybox.width = 10;
mybox.height = 20;
mybox.depth = 15;
// compute volume of box
vol = mybox.width * mybox.height * mybox.depth;
System.out.println("Volume is " + vol);
}
}
```

OUTPUT:

Volume is 3000.0

Program: Java Program to define methods

```
class Test
{
// method definition
```

```
public static void sum()
{
System.out.println("This is a method");
System.out.println(5 + 5);
}
public static void main(String[] args)
{
// method calling
sum();
}
}
```

OUTPUT:

This is a method
10

Program: Java Program to define methods

```
class Test
{
// method definition
public static void printArea(int x, int y) {
System.out.println(x * y);
}
public static void main(String[] args)
{
// calling method
printArea(10, 40);
}
}
```

OUTPUT:

400

Program: Java Program Defining Classes and Objects

//Creating Classes and Objects in Java

//A class is created using the class keyword.

```
class Student
{
```

```
String name;
int roll_no;
}
//let's create an object of this class.
// Student class
class Student
{
String name;
int roll_no;
}
// StrTestPgm (Main) class
class StrTestPgm
{
publicstaticvoid main(String[] args)
{
// creating object st of class Student
Student st = new Student();
}
}
//Any number of objects of a class can be created.
// Student class
class Student
{
String name;
int roll_no;
}
// StrTestPgm (Main) class
class StrTestPgm
{
publicstaticvoid main(String[] args)
{
// creating objects st1 and st2 of class Student
Student st1 = new Student();
Student st2 = new Student();
}
}
```

//Java Attributes

```
// Student class
class Student
{
String name = "John";
}
// StrTestPgm (Main) class
class StrTestPgm
{
publicstaticvoid main(String[] args)
```

```
{
// creating object st of class Student
Student st = new Student();
System.out.println(st.name);
}
}
```

OUTPUT:

John

Program: Java Program assigning values to attributes

```
// Student class
class Student
{
String name;
}
// StrTestPgm (Main) class
class StrTestPgm
{
publicstaticvoid main(String[] args)
{
// creating object st of class Student
Student st = new Student();
// assigning value to attribute name
st.name = "Arun";
System.out.println(st.name);
}
}
```

OUTPUT:

Arun

Program: Java Program Using Classes and Methods

```
// Student class
class Student
{
String name = "Arun";
}
// StrTestPgm (Main) class
class StrTestPgm
{
publicstaticvoid main(String[] args)
{
// creating objects st1 and st2 of class Student
```

```
Student st1 = new Student();
Student st2 = new Student();
System.out.println("Student 1 Name: " + st1.name);
System.out.println("Student 2 Name: " + st2.name);
}
}
```

OUTPUT:

Student 1 Name: John
Student 2 Name: John

Program: Java Program to define different names for both the objects

```
// Student class
class Student
{
String name;
}
// StrTestPgm (Main) class
class StrTestPgm
{
publicstaticvoid main(String[] args)
{
// creating objects of class Student
Student st1 = new Student();
Student st2 = new Student();
// assigning values to attribute name for objects
st1.name = "Arun";
st2.name = "Mary";
System.out.println("Student 1 Name: " + st1.name);
System.out.println("Student 2 Name: " + st2.name);
}
}
```

OUTPUT:

Student 1 Name: Arun
Student 2 Name: Mary

Program : Java Program Using Methods in Class

```
// Student class
class Student
{
String name = "Arun";
void description() {
System.out.println("Is a student");
```

```
}
}
// StrTestPgm (Main) class
class StrTestPgm
{
publicstaticvoid main(String[] args)
{
// creating object st of class Student
Student st = new Student();
// accessing variable name of class
System.out.println(st.name);
// accessing method description of class
st.description();
}
}
```

OUTPUT:

Arun
Is a student

Program : Java Program Using Methods in Class

```
class Student
{
String name;
void setName(String n)
{
name = n;
}
String getName()
{
return name;
}
}
class StrTestPgm
{
publicstaticvoid main(String[] args)
{
Student st = new Student();
st.setName("Tharun");
String st_name = st.getName();
System.out.println("Student Name: " + st_name);
}
}
```

OUTPUT:

Student Name: Tharun

Program: Java Program to define methods

```
class Test {
    public static void printSum(int x, int y) {
    System.out.println(x + y);
    }
    public static void main(String[] args) {
    printSum(100, 5);
    }}
```

OUTPUT:

105

Program: Java Program to Call Methods

```
class Test
    {
    // method definition
    public static void sum()
    {
    System.out.println("This is a method");
    System.out.println(5 + 6);
    }
    public static void main(String[] args)
    {
    System.out.println("Calling method first time");
    // calling method
    sum();
    System.out.println("Calling method second time");
    // calling method
    sum();
    }
    }
```

OUTPUT:

Calling method first time
This is a method
11
Calling method second time
This is a method
11

Program: Java Program to Call Methods Several Times

```
class Test
   {
   // method definition
   public static void printArea(int x, int y)
   {
   System.out.println(x * y);
   }
   public static void main(String[] args)
   {
   printArea(5, 4);
   printArea(10, 8);
   printArea(100, 46);
   printArea(1000, 45);
   }
   }
```

OUTPUT:

```
20
80
4600
45000
```

Program: Java Program to Using Return Statements

```
class Test
   {
   // method definition
   public static int getArea(int x, int y)
   {
   int z = x * y;
   return z;
   }
   public static void main(String[] args)
   {
   // calling method
   int area = getArea(20, 25;
   System.out.println("Area: " + area);
   }
   }
```

OUTPUT:

```
Area: 500
```

Program: Java Program to Using Return Statements

```
class Test
```

```
{
// method definition
public static boolean isEven(int x)
{
if (x % 2 == 0)
{
return true;
}
else
{
return false;
}
}
public static void main(String[] args)
{
int num = 4;
System.out.println("Is number even? " + isEven(num));
}
}
```

OUTPUT:

Is number even? True

Program: Java Program Calling a Method Inside Another Method

```
class Test
{
// method divby2() definition
public static int divby2(int a)
{
if (a % 2 == 0) {
return 1;
}
else {
return 0;
}
}
// method divby6() definition
public static void divby6(int b) {
if (divby2(b) == 1 && b % 3 == 0) {
System.out.println("Yes, the number is divisible by 6.");
}
else
{
System.out.println("No, the number is not divisible by 6.");
}
}
```

```
public static void main(String[] args)
{
divby6(12);
divby6(25);
}
}
```

OUTPUT:

Yes, the number is divisible by 6.
No, the number is not divisible by 6.

Program: Java Program Calling a Method Inside Another Method

```
class Test
{
public static int getSum(int x, int y)
{
return x + y;
}
public static int getProduct(int x, int y)
{
return x * y;
}
public static int getSumOfProduct(int x, int y, int a, int b)
{
int firstProduct = getProduct(x, y);
int secondProduct = getProduct(a, b);
int sumOfProduct = getSum(firstProduct, secondProduct);
return sumOfProduct;
}
public static void main(String[] args)
{
System.out.println(getSumOfProduct(1, 2, 3, 4));
}
}
```

OUTPUT:

14

Program: Java Program Using Inheritance

```
// superclass
class Person
{
publicvoid print1()
{
```

```
System.out.println("I am superclass");
}
}
// subclass
class Student extends Person
{
publicvoid print2()
{
System.out.println("I am subclass");
}
}
class StrTestPgm
{
publicstaticvoid main(String[] args)
{
// creating object of subclass
Student st = new Student();
st.print1();
st.print2();
}
}
```

OUTPUT:

I am superclass
I am subclass

Program: Java Program Using Inheritance

```
// superclass
class Person
{
publicvoid print1()
{
System.out.println("I am superclass");
}
}
// subclass
class Student extends Person
{
publicvoid print2()
{
System.out.println("I am subclass");
}
}
class StrTestPgm
{
publicstaticvoid main(String[] args)
```

```
{
// creating object of superclass
Person p = new Person();
p.print1();
p.print2();
}
}
```

OUTPUT:

```
StrTestPgm.java:21: error: cannot find symbol
    p.print2();
^
symbol: method print2()
location: variable p of type Person
1 error
```

Program: Java Program Using Inheritance

```
// superclass
    class Person
    {
    protected String name;
    protectedvoid display()
    {
    System.out.println("This is a superclass method");
    }
    }
    // subclass
    class Student extends Person
    {
    publicvoid printName()
    {
    System.out.println("Name: " + name); // accessing protected variable of superclass in subclass
    }
    }
    class StrTestPgm
    {
    publicstaticvoid main(String[] args)
    {
    // creating object of subclass
    Student st = new Student();
    // accessing protected variable and method of superclass using object of subclass
    st.name = "Pankaj";
    st.printName();
    }
    }
```

OUTPUT:

Name: Pankaj

Program: Java Program Using Subclass with Constructor

```
// superclass
classPerson
{
public Person()
{
System.out.println("Constructor of parent class");
}
}
// subclass
classStudentextends Person
{
public Student() {
System.out.println("Constructor of child class");
}
}
class StrTestPgm
{
publicstaticvoid main(String[] args)
{
// creating object of subclass
Student st = new Student();
}
}
```

OUTPUT:

Constructor of parent class
Constructor of child class

Program: Java Program Using Inheritance

```
class Shape
{
publicvoid m()
{
System.out.println("This is a Shape");
}
}
class Rectangle extends Shape
{
publicvoid m1()
{
```

```
System.out.println("This is a Rectangle");
}
}
class Square extends Rectangle
{
publicvoid m2()
{
System.out.println("This is a Square");
}
}
class Test
{
publicstaticvoid main(String[] args)
{
Rectangle rec = new Rectangle(); // creating object r of Rectangle
Square squ = new Square(); // creating object s of Square
rec.m();
rec.m1();
System.out.println("****");
squ.m();
squ.m1();
squ.m2();
}
}
```

OUTPUT:

This is a Shape
This is a Rectangle
****
This is a Shape
This is a Rectangle
This is a Square

Program: Java Program Using Inheritance

```
class Shape
{
publicvoid m()
{
System.out.println("This is a Shape");
}
}
class Rectangle extends Shape
{
publicvoid m1()
{
System.out.println("This is a Rectangle");
```

```
}
}
class Circle extends Shape
{
publicvoid m2()
{
System.out.println("This is a Circle");
}
}
class Test
{
publicstaticvoid main(String[ ] args)
{
Rectangle rec = new Rectangle(); // creating object r of Rectangle
Circle cir = new Circle(); // creating object c of Circle
rec.m();
rec.m1();
System.out.println("****");
cir.m();
cir.m2();
}
}
```

OUTPUT:

This is a Shape
This is a Rectangle
****
This is a Shape
This is a Circle

Program: Java Program Using Inheritance

```
// superclass
class Person
{
protected String name;
protectedint age;
publicvoid setPersonDetails(String p_name, int p_age)
{
name = p_name;
age = p_age;
}
publicvoid getPersonDetails()
{
System.out.println("Name: " + name);
System.out.println("Age: " + age);
}
```

```
}
// subclass 1
class Student extends Person
{
privateint marks;
publicvoid setStudentDetails(String s_name, int s_age, int s_marks)
{
setPersonDetails(s_name, s_age);
marks = s_marks;
}
publicvoid getStudentDetails()
{
System.out.println("#### Student Details ####");
getPersonDetails();
System.out.println("Marks: " + marks);
}
}
// subclass 2
class Faculty extends Person
{
privateint salary;
publicvoid setFacultyDetails(String t_name, int t_age, int t_salary)
{
setPersonDetails(t_name, t_age);
salary = t_salary;
}
publicvoid getFacultyDetails()
{
System.out.println("#### Faculty ####");
getPersonDetails();
System.out.println("Salary: " + salary);
}
}
class Test
{
publicstaticvoid main(String[] args)
{
// creating object of subclass Student
Student st = new Student();
st.setStudentDetails("JohnSmith", 20, 84);
st.getStudentDetails();
// creating object of subclass Teacher
Faculty tch = new Faculty();
tch.setFacultyDetails("JulieMathew", 40, 200000);
tch.getFacultyDetails();
}
}
```

OUTPUT:

```
#### Student Details ####
Name: JohnSmith
Age: 20
Marks: 84
#### Faculty Details ####
Name: JulieMathew
Age: 40
Salary: 200000
```

Program: Java Program Using instanceof Example

```
// superclass
    class Rectangle
    {
    }
    // subclass
    class Square extends Rectangle
    {
    }
    class Test
    {
    publicstaticvoid main(String[] args)
    {
    // creating object of superclass
    Rectangle rect = new Rectangle();
    // creating object of subclass
    Square sq = new Square();
    System.out.println(rect instanceof Rectangle);
    System.out.println(sq instanceof Square);
    System.out.println(sq instanceof Rectangle);
    System.out.println(rect instanceof Square);
    }
    }
```

OUTPUT:

```
true
true
true
false
```

Program: Java Program Using Method Overriding

```
class Animal
    {
    publicvoid printSound()
```

```
{
System.out.println("Sound method of parent class");
}
}
class Dog extends Animal
{
publicvoid printSound()
{
System.out.println("Dogs are barking");
}
}
class Test
{
publicstaticvoid main(String[] args)
{
Dog d = new Dog();
d.printSound();
}
}
```

OUTPUT:

Dogs are barking

Program: Java Program, Conditions for Method Overriding in Java

```
class Animal
{
publicvoid printSound()
{
System.out.println("Sound method of parent class");
}
}
class Dog extends Animal
{
publicvoid printSound()
{
System.out.println("Dogs are barking");
}
}
class Cat extends Animal
{
publicvoid printSound()
{
System.out.println("Cats are meowing");
}
}
class Pig extends Animal
```

```
{
publicvoid printSound()
{
System.out.println("Pigs are snorting");
}
}
class Test
{
publicstaticvoid main(String[] args)
{
Dog d = new Dog();
Cat c = new Cat();
Pig p = new Pig();
d.printSound();
c.printSound();
p.printSound();
}
}
```

Output

Dogs are barking
Cats are meowing
Pigs are snorting

Program: Java Program, Conditions for Method Overriding in Java

```
class Animal
{
protectedvoid printSound()
{
System.out.println("Sound method of parent class");
}
}
class Dog extends Animal
{
publicvoid printSound()
{
System.out.println("Dogs bark from Dog class");
}
}
class Test
{
publicstaticvoid main(String[] args)
{
Dog d = new Dog();
d.printSound();
}
}
```

OUTPUT:

Dogs bark from Dog class

Program: Java Program Using super Keyword

Calling Parent Class Methods

```
// superclass
class Person
{
publicvoid message()
{
System.out.println("Person class");
}
}
// subclass
class Student extends Person
{
publicvoid message()
{
System.out.println("Student class");
}
publicvoid display()
{
message();
}
}
class Test
{
publicstaticvoid main(String[] args)
{
Student st = new Student();
st.display();
}
}
```

OUTPUT:

Student class

Program: Java Program Using super Keyword

```
// superclass
class Person
{
publicvoid message()
```

```
{
System.out.println("Person Object");
}
}
// subclass
class Student extends Person
{
publicvoid message()
{
System.out.println("Student Object");
}
publicvoid display()
{
super.message();
}
}
class Test
{
publicstaticvoid main(String[] args)
{
Student st = new Student();
st.display();
}
}
```

OUTPUT:

Person Object

Program: Java Program Accessing Parent Class Attributes

```
// superclass
class Person
{
protected String name = "JohnSmith";
}
// subclass
class Student extends Person
{
private String name = "JulieMathew";
publicvoid display()
{
System.out.println(name);
}
}
class Test
{
publicstaticvoid main(String[] args)
```

```
{
Student st = new Studcnt( );
st.display();
}
}
```

OUTPUT:

JulieMathew

Program: Java Program Accessing Parent Class Attributes

```
// superclass
class Person
{
protected String name = "JohnSmith";
}
// subclass
class Student extends Person
{
private String name = "JulieThomas";
publicvoid display()
{
System.out.println(super.name);
}
}
class Test
{
publicstaticvoid main(String[] args)
{
Student st = new Student();
st.display();
}
}
```

OUTPUT:

JohnSmith

Program: Java Program Using Calling Parent Class Constructor

```
// superclass
class Person
{
public Person()
{
System.out.println("Parent Class Constructor");
}
```

```
}
// subclass
class Student extends Person
{
public Student()
{
super(); // calls the default constructor of the superclass
System.out.println("Child Class Constructor");
}
}
class Test
{
publicstaticvoid main(String[] args)
{
Student st = new Student();
}
}
```

OUTPUT:

```
Parent Class Constructor
Child Class Constructor
```

Program: Java Program Using Calling Parent Class Constructor

```
// superclass
class Person
{
public Person()
{
System.out.println("Parent Class Constructor");
}
}
// subclass
class Student extends Person
{
public Student() {
System.out.println("Child Class Constructor");
}
}
class Test
{
public static void main(String[] args)
{
Student st = new Student();
}
}
```

OUTPUT:

Parent Class Constructor
Child Class Constructor

Program: Java Program Using Inheritance

```
// superclass
class Person
{
protected String name;
public Person()
{
System.out.println("Default constructor of parent class");
}
public Person(String n)
{
name = n;
System.out.println("name: " + name);
}
}
// subclass
class Student extends Person
{
public Student()
{
super("JohnHopkins"); // calls the parameterized constructor of the superclass
System.out.println("Constructor of child class");
}
}
class Test
{
publicstaticvoid main(String[] args)
{
Student st = new Student();
}
}
```

OUTPUT:

name: JohnHopkins
Constructor of child class

Program: Java Program Using Inheritance

```
// superclass
class Person
{
```

```
protected String name;
public Person()
{
System.out.println("Default constructor of parent class");
}
public Person(String n)
{
name = n;
System.out.println("name: " + name);
}
}
// subclass
class Student extends Person
{
public Student()
{
super("JohnVargese"); // calls the parameterized constructor of the superclass
System.out.println("Constructor of child class");
}
}
class Test
{
publicstaticvoid main(String[] args)
{
Student st = new Student();
}
}
```

OUTPUT:

name: JohnVargese
Constructor of child class

Program: Java Program with A Real Life Example of Use of super Keyword

```
// superclass
class Person
{
protected String name;
protectedint age;
public Person(String p_name, int p_age)
{
name = p_name;
age = p_age;
}
publicvoid display()
{
System.out.println("Name: " + name);
```

```
System.out.println("Age: " + age);
}
}
// subclass 1
class Student extends Person
{
privateint marks;
public Student(String s_name, int s_age, int s_marks)
{
super(s_name, s_age);
marks = s_marks;
}
publicvoid display()
{
System.out.println("#### Details of Student ####");
super.display();
System.out.println("Marks: " + marks);
}
}
// subclass 2
class Faculty extends Person
{
privateint salary;
public Faculty(String t_name, int t_age, int t_salary)
{
super(t_name, t_age);
salary = t_salary;
}
publicvoid display() {
System.out.println("#### Details of Faculty ####");
super.display();
System.out.println("Salary: " + salary);
}
}
class Test
{
publicstaticvoid main(String[] args)
{
// creating object of subclass Student
Student st = new Student("John", 20, 84);
st.display();
// creating object of subclass Teacher
Faculty tch = new Faculty("Julie", 30, 300000);
tch.display();
}
}
```

Output

```
    #### Details of Student ####
Name: John
Age: 20
Marks: 84
#### Details of Faculty ####
Name: Julie
Age: 30
Salary: 300000
```

CHAPTER SEVEN

Constructors

Program: Java Program Using Default Constructor

```
/* Here, Box uses a constructor to initialize the
dimensions of a box.
*/
class Box
{
double width;
double height;
double depth;
// This is the constructor for Box.
Box()
{
System.out.println("Constructing Box");
width = 10;
height = 10;
depth = 10;
}
// compute and return volume
double volume()
{
return width * height * depth;
}
}
class BoxDemo6
{
public static void main(String args[])
{
// declare, allocate, and initialize Box objects
Box mybox1 = new Box();
Box mybox2 = new Box();
double vol;
// get volume of first box
vol = mybox1.volume();
System.out.println("Volume is " + vol);
// get volume of second box
vol = mybox2.volume();
```

```
System.out.println("Volume is " + vol);
}
}
```

OUTPUT:

```
Constructing Box
Constructing Box
Volume is 1000.0
Volume is 1000.0
```

Program: Java Program Using Parameterized Constructor

```
/* Here, Box uses a parameterized constructor to
initialize the dimensions of a box.
*/
class Box
{
double width;
double height;
double depth;
// This is the constructor for Box.
Box(double w, double h, double d)
{
width = w;
height = h;
depth = d;
}
// compute and return volume
double volume()
{
return width * height * depth;
}
}
class BoxDemo7
{
public static void main(String args[])
{
// declare, allocate, and initialize Box objects
Box mybox1 = new Box(10, 20, 15);
Box mybox2 = new Box(3, 6, 9);
double vol;
// get volume of first box
vol = mybox1.volume();
System.out.println("Volume is " + vol);
// get volume of second box
vol = mybox2.volume();
System.out.println("Volume is " + vol);
```

```
}
}
```

OUTPUT:

```
Volume is 3000.0
Volume is 162.0
```

Program: Java Program Using Overloaded Constructor

```
/* Here, Box defines three constructors to initialize
the dimensions of a box various ways.
*/
class Box
{
double width;
double height;
double depth;
// constructor used when all dimensions specified
Box(double w, double h, double d)
{
width = w;
height = h;
depth = d;
}
// constructor used when no dimensions specified
Box()
{
width = -1; // use -1 to indicate
height = -1; // an uninitialized
depth = -1; // box
}
// constructor used when cube is created
Box(double len)
{
width = height = depth = len;
}
// compute and return volume
double volume()
{
return width * height * depth;
}
}
class OverloadCons
{
public static void main(String args[])
```

```
{
// create boxes using the various constructors
Box mybox1 = new Box(10, 20, 15);
Box mybox2 = new Box();
Box my cube = new Box(7);
double vol;
// get volume of first box
vol = mybox1.volume();
System.out.println("Volume of mybox1 is " + vol);
// get volume of second box
vol = mybox2.volume();
System.out.println("Volume of mybox2 is " + vol);
// get volume of cube
vol = mycube.volume();
System.out.println("Volume of mycube is " + vol);
}
}
```

OUTPUT:

```
Volume of mybox1 is 3000.0
Volume of mybox2 is -1.0
Volume of mycube is 343.0
```

Program: Java Program Using Methods Inside Class

```
// This program includes a method inside the box class.
class Box
{
double width;
double height;
double depth;
// display volume of a box
void volume()
{
System.out.print("Volume is ");
System.out.println(width * height * depth);
}
}
class BoxDemo3
{
public static void main(String args[])
{
Box mybox1 = new Box();
Box mybox2 = new Box();
// assign values to mybox1's instance variables
mybox1.width = 10;
mybox1.height = 20;
```

```
mybox1.depth = 15;
/* assign different values to mybox2's
instance variables */
mybox2.width = 3;
mybox2.height = 6;
mybox2.depth = 9;
// display volume of first box
mybox1.volume();
// display volume of second box
mybox2.volume();
}
}
```

OUTPUT:

```
Volume is 3000.0
Volume is 162.0
```

Program: Java Program Using return Statement

```
// Now, volume() returns the volume of a box.
class Box
{
double width;
double height;
double depth;
// compute and return volume
double volume()
{
return width * height * depth;
}
}
class BoxDemo4
{
public static void main(String args[])
{
Box mybox1 = new Box();
Box mybox2 = new Box();
double vol;
// assign values to mybox1's instance variables
mybox1.width = 10;
mybox1.height = 20;
mybox1.depth = 15;
/* assign different values to mybox2's
instance variables */
mybox2.width = 3;
mybox2.height = 6;
mybox2.depth = 9;
```

```
// get volume of first box
vol = mybox1.volume();
System.out.println("Volume is " + vol);
// get volume of second box
vol = mybox2.volume();
System.out.println("Volume is " + vol);
}
}
```

OUTPUT:

```
Volume is 3000
Volume is 162
```

Program: Java Program Using Parameterized Method

```
// This program uses a parameterized method.
class Box
{
double width;
double height;
double depth;
// compute and return volume
double volume()
{
return width * height * depth;
}
// sets dimensions of box
void setDim(double w, double h, double d)
{
width = w;
height = h;
depth = d;
}
}
class BoxDemo5
{
public static void main(String args[])
{
Box mybox1 = new Box();
Box mybox2 = new Box();
double vol;
// initialize each box
mybox1.setDim(10, 20, 15);
mybox2.setDim(3, 6, 9);
// get volume of first box
vol = mybox1.volume();
System.out.println("Volume is " + vol);
```

```
// get volume of second box
vol = mybox2.volume();
System.out.println("Volume is " + vol);
}
}
```

OUTPUT:

```
Volume is 3000
Volume is 162
```

Program: Java Program Using 'this' keyword

```
class Student
{
int id;
String name;
student(int id, String name)
{
this.id = id;
this.name = name;
}
void display()
{
System.out.println(id+" "+name);
}
public static void main(String args[])
{
Student stud1 = new Student(01,"Varun");
Student stud2 = new Student(02,"Tharun");
stud1.display();
stud2.display();
}
}
```

OUTPUT:

```
01 Varun
02 Tharun
```

Program: Java Program With Overloaded Methods

```
// Demonstrate method overloading.
class OverloadDemo
{
void test()
{
System.out.println("No parameters");
```

```
}
// Overload test for one integer parameter.
void test(int a)
{
System.out.println("a: " + a);
}
// Overload test for two integer parameters.
void test(int a, int b)
{
System.out.println("a and b: " + a + " " + b);
}
// Overload test for a double parameter
double test(double a)
{
System.out.println("double a: " + a);
return a*a;
}
}
class Overload
{
public static void main(String args[])
{
OverloadDemo ob = new OverloadDemo();
double result;
// call all versions of test()
ob.test();
ob.test(10);
ob.test(10, 20);
result = ob.test(123.25);
System.out.println("Result of ob.test(123.25): " + result);
}
}
```

OUTPUT:

```
No parameters
20
a: 10
a and b: 10 20
double a: 123.25
Result of ob.test(123.25): 15190.5625
```

Program: Java Program Using Constructor

```
class Student
{
String name;
// constructor
```

```
Student()
{
name = "Unknown";
}
void setName(String n)
{
name = n;
}
String getName()
{
return name;
}
}
class StrTestPgm
{
publicstaticvoid main(String[] args)
{
// creating object st of Student class
Student st = new Student();
// printing value of name of st
System.out.println("Student Name: " + st.getName());
// changing value of name of st
st.setName("Venkatesh");
// printing value of name of st
System.out.println("Student Name: " + st.getName());
}
}
```

OUTPUT:

Student Name: Unknown
Student Name: Venkatesh

Program: Java Program Using Constructorclass Student

```
class Student
{
String name;
int age;
// constructor
Student()
{
name = "Unknown";
age = 0;
}
void setDetails(String n, int a)
{
name = n;
```

```
age = a;
}
void printDetails()
{
System.out.println("My name is " + name + " and my age is " + age);
}
}
class StrTestPgm
{
publicstaticvoid main(String[] args)
{
Student st1 = new Student();
Student st2 = new Student();
st1.setDetails("John", 25);
st2.setDetails("Julie", 20);
st1.printDetails();
st2.printDetails();
}
}
```

OUTPUT:

My name is John and my age is 25
My name is Julie and my age is 20

Program: Java Program Using Constructor Having Parameters

```
class Student
{
String name;
int age;
// constructor
Student(String n, int a)
{
name = n;
age = a;
}
void printDetails()
{
System.out.println("My name is " + name + " and my age is " + age);
}
}
class StrTestPgm
{
publicstaticvoid main(String[] args)
{
Student st1 = new Student("Premanand", 25);
Student st2 = new Student("Vargese", 20);
```

```
st1.printDetails();
st2.printDetails();
}
}
```

OUTPUT:

My name is Premanand and my age is 25
My name is Vargese and my age is 20

Program: Java Program Using public and private Modifiers

```
class Student
{
private String name;
privateint age;
// constructor
public Student(String n, int a)
{
name = n;
age = a;
}
publicvoid printDetails()
{
System.out.println("My name is " + name + " and my age is " + age);
}
}
class StrTestPgm
{
publicstaticvoid main(String[] args)
{
Student st1 = new Student("Prabhu", 27);
st1.printDetails();
}
}
```

Output

My name is Prabhu and my age is 27

Program: Java Program Using public and private Modifiers

```
class Student
{
private String name;
privateint age;
// constructor
public Student(String n, int a)
{
name = n;
```

```
age = a;
}
publicvoid printDetails()
{
System.out.println("My name is " + name + " and my age is " + age);
}
}
class StrTestPgm
{
publicstaticvoid main(String[] args)
{
Student st1 = new Student("John", 25);
System.out.println(st1.name);
}
}
```

OUTPUT:

StrTestPgm.java:19: error: name has private access in Student
System.out.println(st1.name); ^
1 error

Program: Java Program Using public and private Modifiers

```
class Rectangle
{
privateint length;
privateint breadth;
public Rectangle(int l, int b)
{
length = l;
breadth = b;
}
publicint getArea()
{
return length * breadth;
}
}
class StrTestPgm
{
publicstaticvoid main(String[] args)
{
Rectangle rect = new Rectangle(2, 4);
System.out.println(rect.getArea());
}
}
```

OUTPUT:

8

Program: Java Program Using Java static elements

```
class Rectangle
{
publicstaticvoid printArea(int l, int b)
{
System.out.println(l * b);
}
}
class StrTestPgm
{
publicstaticvoid main(String[] args)
{
Rectangle.printArea(5, 10);
}
}
```

OUTPUT:

50

Program: Java Program Returning and Passing Object in a Method

```
class Account
{
public int balance;
public Account()
{
balance = 0;
}
public static Account getAcc(Account a, Account b)
{
Account ac = new Account();
ac.balance = a.balance + b.balance;
return ac;
}
}
class StrTestPgm
{
public static void main(String[] args)
{
Account a1 = new Account();
a1.balance = 50;
Account a2 = new Account();
```

```
a2.balance = 60;
Account a3 = Account.getAcc(a1, a2);
System.out.println(a3.balance);
}
}
```

OUTPUT:

110

Program: Java Program Using Array of Objects

```
class Rectangle
{
privateint length;
privateint breadth;
public Rectangle(int l, int b)
{
length = l;
breadth = b;
}
public int getArea()
{
return length * breadth;
}
}
class StrTestPgm
{
public static void main(String[] args) {
Rectangle rect1 = new Rectangle(2, 4); // 1st rectangle
Rectangle rect2 = new Rectangle(4, 5); // 2nd rectangle
System.out.println(rect1.getArea());
System.out.println(rect2.getArea());
}
}
```

OUTPUT:

8
20

Program: Java Program For Creating Array of Objects in Java

```
class Rectangle
{
privateint length;
privateint breadth;
public Rectangle(int l, int b)
```

```
{
length = l;
breadth = b;
}
publicint getArea()
{
return length * breadth;
}
}
class StrTestPgm
{
publicstaticvoid main(String[] args)
{
// declaring array of objects
Rectangle[] rect = new Rectangle[2];
// initializing array
rect[0] = new Rectangle(5, 20);
rect[1] = new Rectangle(10, 5);
for (int i = 0; i < 2; i++) {
System.out.println(rect[i].getArea());
}
}
}
```

Output

100
50

Program: Java Program Using Scanner

```
import java.util.Scanner;
class Student
{
private String name;
privateint marks;
publicvoid setDetails(String n, int m)
{
name = n;
marks = m;
}
publicvoid printDetails()
{
System.out.println("Student Name: " + name);
System.out.println("Marks Obtained: " + marks);
}
}
classStrTestPgm
{
publicstaticvoid main(String[] args)
```

```
{
// declaring array of objects
Student[] st = new Student[5];
// initializing array
Scanner s = new Scanner(System.in);
for (int i = 0; i < 5; i++)
{
System.out.println("Student " + (i + 1));
System.out.println("Enter name");
String name = s.next();
System.out.println("Enter marks");
int marks = s.nextInt();
st[i] = new Student();
st[i].setDetails(name, marks);
}
// printing details of the objects
for (int i = 0; i < 5; i++) {
st[i].printDetails();
}
}
}
```

OUTPUT:

```
Student 1
Enter name
JimJack
Enter marks
54
Student 2
Enter name
KarlMarx
Enter marks
45
Student 3
Enter name
JanetJulie
Enter marks
47
Student 4
Enter name
JamesPeterson
Enter marks
23
Student 5
Enter name
McDonald
Enter marks
```

87
Student 1
Student Name : JimJack
Marks Obtained : 54
Student 2
Student Name : KarlMarx
Marks Obtained : 45
Student 3
Student Name : JanetJulie
Marks Obtained: 47
Student 4
Student Name : JamesPeterson
Marks Obtained : 23
Student 5
Student Name : McDonald
Marks Obtained: 87

Program: Java Constructor Overloading

```
class Rectangle
{
privateint length;
privateint breadth;
public Rectangle(int side)
{
length = side;
breadth = side;
}
public Rectangle(int l, int b)
{
length = l;
breadth = b;
}
publicint getArea()
{
return length * breadth;
}
}
class StrTestPgm
{
publicstaticvoid main(String[] args)
{
Rectangle rect = new Rectangle(4, 5);
Rectangle sq = new Rectangle(5);
System.out.println(rect.getArea());
System.out.println(sq.getArea());
}
}
```

OUTPUT:

```
20
25
```

Program: Java Program Using Access Modifiers

//Java Public Access Modifier

```
class Student
{
// public variable
public String name;
// constructor
public Student(String n)
{
name = n;
}
// public method
publicvoid printDetails()
{
System.out.println("This is a public method");
}
}
class StrTestPgm
{
publicstaticvoid main(String[] args)
{
Student st = new Student("JohnSmith");
// accessing public variable
System.out.println(st.name);
// accessing public method
st.printDetails();
}
}
```

OUTPUT:

```
JohnSmith
This is a public method
```

Program: Java Program Using Access Modifiers

//Java Public Access Modifier

```
class Student
{
public String name;
public Student(String n)
{
name = n;
}
publicvoid printDetails()
{
System.out.println("This is a public method");
}
}
class StrTestPgm
{
publicstaticvoid main(String[] args)
{
Student st = new Student("JohnHops");
System.out.println(st.name);
st.printDetails();
}
}
```

OUTPUT:

JohnHops
This is a public method

Program: Java Program Using Access Modifiers

//Java Private Access Modifier

```
class Student
{
// private variable
private String name;
}
class StrTestPgm
{
publicstaticvoid main(String[] args)
{
Student st = new Student();
// accessing private variable
st.name = "John";
}
}
```

OUTPUT:

```
StrTestPgm.java:11: error: name has private access in Student
st.name = "John";
^
1 error
```

Program: Java Program Using Access Modifiers

//Java Private Access Modifier

```
class Student
{
// private variable
private String name;
//public method
publicvoid setName(String n)
{
name = n;
}
// public method
public String getName()
{
return name;
}
}
class StrTestPgm
{
publicstaticvoid main (String[] args)
{
Student st = new Student();
// accessing public method
st.setName("JohnSmith");
// accessing public method
System.out.println(st.getName());
}
}
```

OUTPUT:

```
JohnSmith
```

Program: Java Program Using Constructors

```
class Student
{
// constructor
```

```
public Student()
{
System.out.println("I am constructor");
}
// block
{
System.out.println("I am block");
}
}
class Test
{
public static void main(String[] args)
{
Student st1 = new Student();
Student st2 = new Student();
}
}
```

OUTPUT:

I am block
I am constructor
I am block
I am constructor

Program: Java Program Using Constructors and static Block

```
class Student
{
// static block
static
{
System.out.println("I am static block");
}
// constructor
public Student()
{
System.out.println("I am constructor");
}
}
class Test
{
public static void main(String[] args)
{
Student st1 = new Student();
Student st2 = new Student();
}
}
```

OUTPUT:

I am static block
I am constructor
I am constructor

Program: Java Program Using Constructors

```
class Student
    {
    String name;
    static String college;
    static {
    college = "IIT";
    }
    public Student(String n)
    {
    name = n;
    }
    public void printDetails()
    {
    System.out.println("Name: " + name + ", College: " + college);
    }
    }
    class Test
    {
    public static void main(String[] args)
    {
    Student st1 = new Student("John");
    Student st2 = new Student("Julie");
    st1.printDetails();
    st2.printDetails();
    }
    }
    Output
    Name: John, College: IIT
Name: Julie, College: IIT
```

Program: Java Program Using this Keyword

```
//Accessing Current Class Attributes
    class Account
    {
    String name;
    int balance;
    Account(String n, int b)
    {
```

```
name = n;
balance = b;
}
void printInfo()
{
System.out.println("Name: " + name + ", Balance: " + balance);
}
}
class Test
{
public static void main(String[] args)
{
Account ac = new Account("Peterson", 7000);
ac.printInfo();
}
}
```

OUTPUT:

Name: Peterson, Balance: 7000

Program: Java Program Using Constructors

```
class Account
{
String name;
int balance;
Account(String name, int balance)
{
name = name;
balance = balance;
}
void printInfo()
{
System.out.println("Name: " + name + ", Balance: " + balance);
}
}
class Test
{
public static void main(String[] args) {
Account ac = new Account("David Peter", 15000);
ac.printInfo();
}
}
```

OUTPUT:

Name: null, Balance: 0

Program: Java Program Using Constructors

```
class Account
    {
    String name;
    int balance;
    Account(String name, int balance)
    {
    this.name = name;
    this.balance = balance;
    }
    void printInfo()
    {
    System.out.println("Name: " + name + ", Balance: " + balance);
    }
    }
    class Test
    {
    public static void main(String[] args)
    {
    Account ac = new Account("Peterson", 50000);
    ac.printInfo();
    }
    }
```

OUTPUT:

Name: Peterson, Balance: 50000

Program: Java Program Calling Current Class Methods

```
class Method
    {
    void method1()
    {
    System.out.println("This is method 1");
    }
    void method2()
    {
    this.method1();
    }
    }
    class Test
    {
    public static void main(String[] args)
    {
    Method m = new Method();
```

```
m.method2();
}
}
```

OUTPUT:

This is method 1

Program: Java Program Using Constructors

```
class Method
{
void method1()
{
System.out.println("This is method 1");
}
void method2()
{
method1();
}
}
class Test
{
public static void main(String[] args)
{
Method m = new Method();
m.method2();
}
}
```

OUTPUT:

This is method 1

Program: Java Program Calling Current Class Constructor

```
class Account
{
String name;
int balance;
Account(String n)
{
name = n;
System.out.println("This is a constructor with single parameter");
}
Account(String n, int b)
{
this(n);
```

```
balance = b;
}
void printInfo()
{
System.out.println("Name: " + name + ", Balance: " + balance);
}
}
class Test
{
public static void main(String[] args)
{
Account ac = new Account("David Peter", 15000);
ac.printInfo();
}
}
```

OUTPUT:

This is a constructor with single parameter
Name: DavidPeter, Balance: 15000

```
class Rectangle
{
private int length;
private int breadth;
public Rectangle(int l, int b)
{
length = l;
breadth = b;
}
public Rectangle(int side)
{
this(side, side);
}
public int getArea()
{
return length * breadth;
}
}
class Test
{
public static void main(String[] args)
{
Rectangle rect = new Rectangle(4, 5);
Rectangle sq = new Rectangle(5);
System.out.println(rect.getArea());
System.out.println(sq.getArea());
}
}
```

OUTPUT:

20
25

Program: Java Program for Passing and Returning Class Object

```
class Rectangle
{
int length, breadth;
Rectangle(int l, int b)
{
length = l;
breadth = b;
}
Rectangle getObj()
{
return this;
}
}
class Test
{
public static void main(String[] args)
{
Rectangle r1 = new Rectangle(25, 40);
Rectangle r2;
r2 = r1.getObj();
System.out.println("length: " + r1.length + " breadth: " + r1.breadth);
System.out.println("length: " + r2.length + " breadth: " + r2.breadth);
}
}
```

OUTPUT:

length: 25 breadth: 40
length: 25 breadth: 40

Program: Java Program Using Constructors

```
class Method
{
void method1(Method m1)
{
System.out.println("This is method 1");
}
void method2()
{
```

```
method1(this);
}
}
class Test
{
public static void main(String[] args)
{
Method m = new Method();
m.method2();
}
}
```

OUTPUT:

This is method 1

Program: Java Program Using final Keyword

```
//Java final Variable
class Student
{
// defining a blank final variable
private final int roll;
public Student(int r)
{
// initializing the blank final variable
roll = r;
}
public void displayRoll()
{
System.out.println(roll);
}
}
class Test
{
public static void main(String[] args)
{
Student s1 = new Student(1);
Student s2 = new Student(2);
s1.displayRoll();
s2.displayRoll();
}
}
```

OUTPUT:

1
2

CHAPTER EIGHT

Abstract classes and methods- final methods

Program: Java Program Using Abstraction

```
// abstract class
abstractclass Animal
{
// abstract method
publicabstractvoid printSound();
// regular method
publicvoid displayInfo()
{
System.out.println("I am an Animal");
}
}
// subclass
class Fox extends Animal
{
//implementing abstract method
publicvoid printSound()
{
System.out.println("Fox Howls");
}
}
class Test
{
publicstaticvoid main(String[] args)
{
Fox d = new Fox();
d.printSound();
d.displayInfo();
}
}
```

OUTPUT:

Fox Howls
I am an Animal

Program: Java Program Using Abstract Class

```
// abstract class
abstractclass Animal
{
// abstract method
publicabstractvoid printSound();
}
// subclass 1
class Lion extends Animal
{
//implementing abstract method
publicvoid printSound()
{
System.out.println("Lions Roar");
}
}
// subclass 2
class Cat extends Animal
{
//implementing abstract method
publicvoid printSound()
{
System.out.println("\nCats Meow");
}
}
// subclass 3
class Monkey extends Animal
{
//implementing abstract method
publicvoid printSound()
{
System.out.println("Monkeys whoop");
}
}
class Test
{
publicstaticvoid main(String[] args) {
Lion d = new Lion();
Cat c = new Cat();
Monkey m = new Monkey();
d.printSound();
c.printSound();
m.printSound();
}
```

```
}
```

OUTPUT:

Lions Roar
Cats Meow
Monkeys whoop

Program: Java Program Using Abstract Classes

```
abstractclass Vehicle
{
abstractvoid printPrice();
}
abstractclass TwoWheeler extends Vehicle
{
abstractvoid printType();
}
abstractclass FourWheeler extends Vehicle
{
}
abstractclass Bike extends TwoWheeler
{
abstractvoid printMileage();
}
abstractclass Bicycle extends TwoWheeler {
abstractvoid hasBasket(boolean basket);
}
// class Yamaha inheriting abstract class Bike
class Yamaha extends Bike
{
publicvoid printPrice()
{
System.out.println("Price: 145300");
}
publicvoid printType()

{
System.out.println("This is a Bike");
}
publicvoid printMileage()
{
System.out.println("Mileage: 59");
}
publicvoid printBrand()
{
System.out.println("Brand: Yamaha");
}
```

```
}
// class Bajaj inheriting abstract class Bike
class Bajaj extends Bike
{
publicvoid printPrice()
{
System.out.println("Price: 85536");
}
publicvoid printType()
{
System.out.println("This is a Bike");
}
publicvoid printMileage()
{
System.out.println("Mileage: 50");
}
publicvoid printBrand()
{
System.out.println("Brand: Bajaj");
}
}
class Test
{
publicstaticvoid main(String[] args)
{
Yamaha y = new Yamaha();
Bajaj b = new Bajaj();
y.printType();
y.printBrand();
y.printMileage();
y.printPrice();
System.out.println("########");
b.printType();
b.printBrand();
b.printMileage();
b.printPrice();
}
}
```

OUTPUT:

```
This is a Bike
Brand: Yamaha
Mileage: 59
Price: 145300
########
This is a Bike
Brand: Bajaj
```

Mileage: 50
Price: 85536

Java Interface

```
// interface
interface Walk
{
void walk();
}
// class Dog implements interface Walk
class Dog implements Walk
{
publicvoid walk()
{
System.out.println("A dog walks for 10 hours in a day");
}
}
class Test
{
publicstaticvoid main(String[] args)
{
Dog d = new Dog();
d.walk();
}
}
```

OUTPUT:

A dog walks for 10 hours in a day

CHAPTER NINE

Interfaces

Programs: Java Programs on Interface

```
interface Shape
    {
    void getArea(int length, int breadth);
    }
    // implement the Rectangle interface
    class Rectangle implements Shape
    {
    // implementation of abstract method
    public void getArea(int length, int breadth)
    {
    System.out.println("The area of the rectangle is " + (length * breadth));
    }
    }
    class Main
    {
    public static void main(String[] args)
    {
    Rectangle r1 = new Rectangle();
    r1.getArea(5, 6);
    }
    }
```

OUTPUT:

The area of the rectangle is 30

Programs: Java Programs on Interface

```
// create an interface
    interface Sentence
    {
    void getName(String name);
    }
    // class implements interface
    class Sample implements Sentence
```

```
{
// implementation of abstract method
public void getName(String name)
{
System.out.println("Sample Sentence: " + name);
}
}
class Main
{
public static void main(String[] args)
{
SampleSentence Sentence = new SampleSentence();
Sentence.getName("Java");
}
}
```

OUTPUT:

Sample Sentence: Java

Programs: Java Programs on Interface

```
import java.io.*;
// A simple interface
interface In1
{
// public, static and final
final int a = 10;
// public and abstract
void display();
}
// A class that implements the interface.
class TestClass implements In1
{
// Implementing the capabilities of
// interface.
public void display(){
System.out.println("Java");
}
// Driver Code
public static void main(String[] args)
{
TestClass t = new TestClass();
t.display();
System.out.println(a);
}
}
```

OUTPUT:

```
Java
   10
```

Programs: Java Programs with Default Method in Java Interface

```
interface Shape
{
void getArea();
// default method
default void getSides() {
System.out.println("Get sides of a Shape.");
}
}
// implements the interface
class Rectangle implements Shape
{
public void getArea() {
int length = 10;
int breadth = 5;
int area = length * breadth;
System.out.println("The area of the rectangle is " + area);
}
// overrides the getSides()
public void getSides() {
System.out.println("It has 4 sides.");
}
}
// implements the interface
class Square implements Shape
{
public void getArea()
{
int length = 10;
int area = length * length;
System.out.println("The area of the square is " + area);
}
}
class Main
{
public static void main(String[] args)
{
// create an object of Rectangle
Rectangle r1 = new Rectangle();
r1.getArea();
r1.getSides();
// create an object of Square
```

```
Square s1 = new Square();
s1.getArea();
s1.getSides();
}
}
```

OUTPUT:

```
The area of the rectangle is 50
It has 4 sides.
The area of the square is 100
It has 4 sides.
```

Programs: Java Programs with Default Method in Java Interface

```
// To use the sqrt function
import java.lang.Math;
interface Shape {
void getArea();
// calculate the perimeter of a Shape
default void getPerimeter(int... sides)
{
int perimeter = 0;
for (int side: sides) {
perimeter += side;
}
System.out.println("Perimeter: " + perimeter);
}
}
class Triangle implements Shape
{
private int a, b, c;
private double s, area;
// initializing sides of a triangle
Triangle(int a, int b, int c)
{
this.a = a;
this.b = b;
this.c = c;
s = 0;
}
// calculate the area of a triangle
public void getArea()
{
s = (double) (a + b + c)/2;
area = Math.sqrt(s*(s-a)*(s-b)*(s-c));
System.out.println("Area: " + area);
}
```

```
}
class Main
{
public static void main(String[] args)
{
Triangle t1 = new Triangle(2, 3, 4);
// calls the method of the Triangle class
t1.getArea();
// calls the method of Shape
t1.getPerimeter(5, 10, 15);
}
}
```

OUTPUT:

```
Area: 2.9047375096555625
Perimeter: 30
```

Program: Java Program Using Interfaces

```
// interface
interface Servicing
{
// abstract method
int getServiceTime();
}
// class implements interface
class Car implements Servicing
{
//implementing abstract method
publicint getServiceTime()
{
return 2;
}
}
// class implements interface
class Bike implements Servicing
{
//implementing abstract method
publicint getServiceTime()
{
return 3;
}
}
class Test
{
publicstaticvoid main(String[] args)
{
```

```
Car c = new Car();
Bike b = new Bike();
System.out.println(c.getServiceTime());
System.out.println(b.getServiceTime());
}
}
```

OUTPUT:

2
3

Program: Java Program with a Real Life Example of Interface

```
//class inherits multiple interfaces
// interface Fly
interface Fly
{
void fly();
}
// interface Walk
interface Walk
{
void walk();
}
// class Sparrow implements interfaces Fly and Walk
class Sparrow implements Fly, Walk
{
publicvoid fly()
{
System.out.println("Sparrows can fly");
}
publicvoid walk()
{
System.out.println("Sparrows can walk");
}
}
// class HummingBird implements interface Fly
class HummingBird implements Fly
{
publicvoid fly()
{
System.out.println("Humming Birds can fly");
}
}
class Test
{
publicstaticvoid main(String[] args)
```

```
{
Sparrow s = new Sparrow();
HummingBird hb = new HummingBird();
s.fly();
s.walk();
hb.fly();
}
}
```

OUTPUT:

Sparrows can fly
Sparrows can walk
Humming Birds can fly

Program: Java Program Using Interface

```
// interface 1
interface Frontend
{
void displayFrontend();
}
// interface 2
interface Backend
{
void displayBackend();
}
// class implements interface 1 and interface 2
class Developer implements Frontend, Backend
{
publicvoid displayFrontend()
{
System.out.println("I code in React");
}
publicvoid displayBackend()
{
System.out.println("I code in Django");
}
}
class Test
{
publicstaticvoid main(String[] args)
{
Developer dev = new Developer();
dev.displayFrontend();
dev.displayBackend();
}
}
```

OUTPUT:

I code in React
I code in Django

CHAPTER TEN

Inner classes

Java Nested and Inner Class

Program : Java Program For Non-Static Nested Class (Inner Class)

```
class CPU {
double price;
// nested class
class Processor{
    // members of nested class
double cores;
String manufacturer;
    double getCache(){
return 4.3;
}
}
    // nested protected class
protected class RAM{
    // members of protected nested class
double memory;
String manufacturer;
    double getClockSpeed(){
return 5.5;
}
}
}
    public class Main {
public static void main(String[] args) {
    // create object of Outer class CPU
CPU cpu = new CPU();
    // create an object of inner class Processor using outer class
CPU.Processor processor = cpu.new Processor();
    // create an object of inner class RAM using outer class CPU
CPU.RAM ram = cpu.new RAM();
System.out.println("Processor Cache = " + processor.getCache());
System.out.println("Ram Clock speed = " + ram.getClockSpeed());
}
```

```
}
```

OUTPUT:

Processor Cache = 4.3
Ram Clock speed = 5.5

Program : Java Program For Accessing Members of Outer Class Within Inner Class

```
class Car {
String carName;
String carType;
    // assign values using constructor
public Car(String name, String type) {
this.carName = name;
this.carType = type;
}
    // private method
private String getCarName() {
return this.carName;
}
    // inner class
class Engine {
String engineType;
void setEngine() {
    // Accessing the carType property of Car
if(Car.this.carType.equals("4WD")){
    // Invoking method getCarName() of Car
if(Car.this.getCarName().equals("Crysler")) {
this.engineType = "Smaller";
} else {
this.engineType = "Bigger";
}
    }else{
this.engineType = "Bigger";
}
}
String getEngineType(){
return this.engineType;
}
}
}
    public class Main {
public static void main(String[] args) {
    // create an object of the outer class Car
Car car1 = new Car("Mazda", "8WD");
    // create an object of inner class using the outer class
Car.Engine engine = car1.new Engine();
```

```
engine.setEngine();
System.out.println("Engine Type for 8WD= " + engine.getEngineType());
    Car car2 = new Car("Crysler", "4WD");
Car.Engine c2engine = car2.new Engine();
c2engine.setEngine();
System.out.println("Engine Type for 4WD = " + c2engine.getEngineType());
}
}
```

OUTPUT:

Program : Java Program For Accessing Inner Class Code From Outer Class Static Area

```
public class Outer {
    class Inner {
    public void add(int a, int b) {
    System.out.println(a+b);
    }
    }
    //Accessing iiner calss method inside Outer class from main method
    public static void main(String[] args) {
    //Inner inner = new Inner(); not possible this in static area
    // First way
    Outer outer = new Outer();
    Inner inner = outer.new Inner();
    inner.add(20, 30);
    // Second way (just simplification of first way)
    new Outer().new Inner().add(30, 40);
    }
    }
```

OUTPUT:

```
50
    70
```

Program : Java Program For Accessing Inner Class Code From Instance Area Of Outer Class

```
public class Outer {
    class Inner {
    public void add(int a, int b) {
    System.out.println(a+b);
    }
    }
    // Outer class instance method
    public void deposit(int a, int b) {
    Inner inner = new Inner();
```

```
inner.add(a, b);
}
public static void main(String[] args) {
// First way
Outer outer = new Outer();
outer.deposit(10, 20);
outer.deposit(40, 60);
}
}
```

OUTPUT:

30
100

Program : Java Program For Accessing Inner Class Code From Out Side Of Outer Class

```
public class Outer {
class Inner {
public void add(int a, int b) {
System.out.println(a+b);
}
}
}
public class TestInner {
public static void main(String[] args) {
// Calling inner class add method fromm out side class
new Outer().new Inner().add(20, 30);
new TestInner().deposite(30, 40);
}
public void deposite(int a, int b) {
new Outer().new Inner().add(a, b);
}
}
```

OUTPUT:

50
70

Program : Java Program For Static Inner Class

```
class MotherBoard {
// static nested class
static class USB{
int usb2 = 2;
int usb3 = 1;
int getTotalPorts(){
```

```
return usb2 + usb3;
}
}
    }
public class Main {
public static void main(String[] args) {
    // create an object of the static nested class
// using the name of the outer class
MotherBoard.USB usb = new MotherBoard.USB();
System.out.println("Total Ports = " + usb.getTotalPorts());
}
}
```

OUTPUT:

```
Total Ports = 3
```

Program : Java Program For Accessing Members Of Outer Class Inside Static Inner Class

```
class MotherBoard {
String model;
public MotherBoard(String model) {
this.model = model;
}
    // static nested class
static class USB{
int usb2 = 2;
int usb3 = 1;
int getTotalPorts(){
// accessing the variable model of the outer classs
if(MotherBoard.this.model.equals("MSI")) {
return 4;
}
else {
return usb2 + usb3;
}
}
}
}
public class Main {
public static void main(String[] args) {
    // create an object of the static nested class
MotherBoard.USB usb = new MotherBoard.USB();
System.out.println("Total Ports = " + usb.getTotalPorts());
}
}
```

OUTPUT:

error: non-static variable this cannot be referenced from a static context

Program : Java Program For Program to check for nested inner classes

```
// Java Program to Check if a Given Class is an Inner Class
    // Importing package where Modifier is defined
import java.lang.reflect.Modifier;
    class GFG {
    // Main driver method
public static void main(String[] args)
{
    // Creating as GFG class object
GFG gfg = new GFG();
    // Creating a InnerClass object
InnerClass innerClass = gfg.new InnerClass();
    // Creating a Static Nested Class object
StaticNestedClass statNested
= new StaticNestedClass();
    // getClass() method of an object returns a
// java.lang.Class instance representing the class
// of the object
Class classInstance1 = innerClass.getClass();
Class classInstance2 = statNested.getClass();
    // Checking if the given classes are nested
    // getEnclosinglClass() of Class instance returns a
// class object representing the immediate enclosing
// class of the instance
    boolean isNested1
= classInstance1.getEnclosingClass() != null;
// classInstance1() method returns a Class object
    // If the specified class is a top-level class, then
// it would returns null
    boolean isNested2
= classInstance2.getEnclosingClass() != null;
    // Check if the given classes are static
    // getModifiers() method of a class returns the
// modifiers of the class encoded as an integer
    // Modifiers.isStatic returns true if the class
// has a static modifier elsereturns false
boolean isStatic1 = Modifier.isStatic(
classInstance1.getModifiers());
boolean isStatic2 = Modifier.isStatic(
classInstance2.getModifiers());
    // If the given classes are nested and non-static,
// then given classes are surely inner classes
```

```
    // Display message
System.out.println(
"Is innerClass an inner class object? : "
+ (isNested1 && !isStatic1));
    // Display message
System.out.println(
"Is statNested an inner class object? : "
+ (isNested2 && !isStatic2));
}
    // Inner Class
class InnerClass {
}
    // Static nested class
static class StaticNestedClass {
}
}
```

OUTPUT:

Is innerClass an inner class object? : true
Is statNested an inner class object? : false

Program : Java Program For Understand Anonymous Inner Class in Java

```
package Demo;
    abstract class Animal
    {
    abstract void cat ();
    }
    class AnonymousInnerClass
    {
    public static void main (String args[])
    {
    Animal p = new Animal ()
    {
    void cat ()
    {
    System.out.println ("Cat is an Animal.");
    }
    };
    p.dog ();
    }
    }
```

OUTPUT:

Cat is an Animal.

CHAPTER ELEVEN

Exceptions

Programs: Java Programs on Errors and Exceptions

```
class Test {
    publicstaticvoid main(String[] args) {
    System.out.println("Java")
    }
    }
```

OUTPUT:

```
Test.java:3: error: ';' expected
System.out.println("Java")
^
1 error
```

Programs: Java Programs on Exceptions in Java

```
classTest {
    publicstaticvoid main(String[] args) {
    System.out.println("Java")
    }
    }
```

OUTPUT:

```
Test.java:3: error: ';' expected
System.out.println("Java")
^
1 error
    class Test {
    publicstaticvoid main(String[] args) {
    int a = 1, b = 2, c = 3;
    a * b = c;
    }
    }
```

OUTPUT:

```
Test.java:4: error: unexpected type
a*b = c;
^
required: variable
found: value
1 error
```

Programs: Java Programs on Unchecked Exceptions

Example 1

```
class Test {
    publicstaticvoid main(String[] args) {
    int a = 10, b = 0;
    int c = a / b;
    }
    }
```

OUTPUT:

```
Exception in thread "main" java.lang.ArithmeticException: / by zero
at Test.main(Test.java:4)
```

Example 2

```
class Test {
    publicstaticvoid main(String[] args) {
    int[] arr = newint[5];
    System.out.println(arr[10]);
    }
    }
```

OUTPUT:

```
Exception in thread "main" java.lang.ArrayIndexOutOfBoundsException: 10
at Test.main(Test.java:4)
```

Programs: Java Programs on Java Exception Handling

```
import java.util.Scanner;
    class Test {
    publicstaticvoid main(String[] args) {
    Scanner s = new Scanner(System.in);
    System.out.println("Please enter a number");
    int num1 = s.nextInt();
```

```
int num2 = 10 / num1;
System.out.println(num2);
}
}
```

OUTPUT:

Please enter a number 0
Exception in thread "main" java.lang.ArithmeticException: / by zero
at Test.main(Test.java:10)

Programs: Java Programs On Try Block and Catch Block

Example 1

```
import java.util.Scanner;
class Test {
publicstaticvoid main(String[] args) {
Scanner s = new Scanner(System.in);
System.out.println("Please enter a number");
int num1 = s.nextInt();
// try block
try {
int num2 = 10 / num1;
System.out.println(num2);
} // catch block
catch (Exception e) {
System.out.println("Please enter the correct input");
}
System.out.println("This statement is outside try-catch blocks.");
}
}
```

OUTPUT:

Please enter a number 0
Please enter the correct input
This statement is outside try-catch blocks.

Example 2

```
import java.util.Scanner;
class Test {
publicstaticvoid main(String[] args) {
Scanner s = new Scanner(System.in);
System.out.println("Please enter a number");
int num1 = s.nextInt();
```

```
// try block
try {
int num2 = 10 / num1;
System.out.println(num2);
} // catch block
catch (Exception e) {
System.out.println("Please enter the correct input");
}
System.out.println("This statement is outside try-catch blocks.");
}
}
```

OUTPUT:

Please enter a number 2
5
This statement is outside try-catch blocks.

Example 3

```
class Test {
  publicstaticvoid main(String[] args) {
  int arr[] = newint[10];
  try {
  arr[15] = 10;
  } catch (ArrayIndexOutOfBoundsException e) {
  System.out.println("Exception: " + e);
  System.out.println("Please enter the correct input");
  }
  }
  }
```

OUTPUT:

Exception: java.lang.ArrayIndexOutOfBoundsException: Index 15 out of bounds for length 10
Please enter the correct input

Example 4

```
class Test {
  publicstaticvoid main(String[] args) {
  int arr[] = newint[10];
  try {
  arr[15] = 10;
  } catch (ArrayIndexOutOfBoundsException e) {
  System.out.println("Exception: " + e.getMessage());
  System.out.println("Wrong index of array!");
  }
```

```
}
}
```

OUTPUT:

Exception: Index 15 out of bounds for length 10
Wrong index of array!

Programs: Java Programs on Handling A Specific Exception

Example 1

```
import java.util.Scanner;
class Test {
publicstaticvoid main(String[] args) {
Scanner s = new Scanner(System.in);
System.out.println("Please enter a number");
int num1 = s.nextInt();
try {
int num2 = 10 / num1;
System.out.println(num2);
} catch (ArithmeticException e) {
System.out.println("Please enter the correct input");
}
System.out.println("This statement is outside try-catch blocks.");
}
}
```

OUTPUT:

Please enter a number 0
Please enter the correct input
This statement is outside try-catch blocks.

Example 2

```
class Test {
publicstaticvoid main(String[] args) {
int arr[] = newint[10];
try {
arr[15] = 10;
} catch (ArithmeticException e) {
System.out.println("Please enter the correct input");
}
System.out.println("This statement is outside try-catch blocks.");
}
}
```

OUTPUT:

Exception in thread "main" java.lang.ArrayIndexOutOfBoundsException: 15
at Test.main(Test.java:6)

Example 3

```
import java.util.Scanner;
    class Test {
    publicstaticvoid main(String[] args) {
    Scanner s = new Scanner(System.in);
    System.out.println("Please enter a number");
    int num = s.nextInt();
    int arr[] = newint[10];
    try {
    arr[num] = 10 / num;
    System.out.println(arr[num]);
    } catch (NullPointerException e) {
    System.out.println("NullPointerException error");
    } catch (ArithmeticException | ArrayIndexOutOfBoundsException e) {
    System.out.println("Please enter the correct input");
    } catch (Exception e) {
    System.out.println("Some error occurred");
    }
    }
    }
```

OUTPUT:

Please enter a number 15
Please enter the correct input

Example 4

```
class Test {
    publicstaticvoid main(String[] args) {
    int arr[] = newint[10];
    try {
    arr[5] = 10 / 0;
    } catch (ArithmeticException e1) {
    System.out.println("Exception: " + e1.getMessage());
    } catch (ArrayIndexOutOfBoundsException e2) {
    System.out.println("Exception: " + e2.getMessage());
    }
    }
    }
```

Output

Exception: / by zero

Programs: Java Programs On Finally

Example 1

```
class Test {
    publicstaticvoid main(String[] args) {
    try {
    int num = 10 / 0;
    System.out.println(num);
    } catch (ArithmeticException e) {
    System.out.println("Number is divided by zero!");
    } catch (ArrayIndexOutOfBoundsException e) {
    System.out.println("Wrong index of array!");
    } catch (Exception e) {
    System.out.println("Some error occurred");
    } finally {
    System.out.println("finally");
    }
    System.out.println("This statement is outside try-catch-finally blocks.");
    }
    }
```

OUTPUT:

Number is divided by zero!
finally
This statement is outside try-catch-finally blocks.

Example2

```
class Test {
    publicstaticvoid main(String[] args) {
    try {
    int num = 10 / 0;
    System.out.println(num);
    } finally {
    System.out.println("finally");
    }
    }
    }
```

OUTPUT:

Exception in thread "main" java.lang.ArithmeticException: / by zero
at Test.main(Test.java:4)

Programs: Java Programs On Throw

Example 1

```
import java.util.Scanner;
    class Test {
    publicstaticvoid main(String[] args) {
    Scanner s = new Scanner(System.in);
    System.out.println("Please enter your roll number");
    int roll = s.nextInt();
    if (roll < 0) {
    thrownew ArithmeticException("Roll number can't be negative");
    } else {
    System.out.println("Valid roll number");
    }
    }
    }
```

OUTPUT:

Please enter your roll number -5
Exception in thread "main" java.lang.ArithmeticException: Roll number can't be negative
at Main.main(Main.java:10)

Example 2

```
import java.util.Scanner;
    class Test {
    publicstaticvoid main(String[] args) {
    Scanner s = new Scanner(System.in);
    System.out.println("Please enter your roll number");
    int roll = s.nextInt();
    try {
    if (roll < 0)
    {
    thrownew ArithmeticException("The number entered is not positive"
    );
    }
    else
    {
    System.out.println("Valid roll number");
    }
    } catch (ArithmeticException e)
```

```
{
System.out.println("An exception is thrown");
System.out.println(e.getMessage());
}
}
}
```

OUTPUT:

Please enter your roll number
-5
An exception is thrown
The number entered is not positive

Example 3

```
import java.util.Scanner;
class Test {
publicstaticvoid main(String[] args) {
Scanner s = new Scanner(System.in);
System.out.println("Please enter your age");
int age = s.nextInt();
try {
if (age < 5) {
thrownew ArithmeticException(
"Not allowed! Your age is less than 5"
);
} elseif (age > 20)
{
thrownew ArithmeticException(
"Not allowed! Your age is greater than 20"
);
}
else
{
System.out.println("Welcome!");
}
} catch (ArithmeticException e) {
System.out.println("An exception is thrown");
System.out.println(e.getMessage());
}
}
}
```

OUTPUT:

Please enter your age
26

An exception is thrown
Not allowed! Your age is greater than 20

Example 4

```
import java.util.Scanner;
   class Test {
   publicstaticvoid main(String[] args) {
   Scanner s = new Scanner(System.in);
   System.out.println("Please enter your roll number");
   int roll = s.nextInt();
   try {
   if (roll < 0) {
   thrownew Exception("The number entered is not positive");
   } else
   {
   System.out.println("Valid roll number");
   }
   } catch (Exception e)
   {
   System.out.println("An exception is thrown");
   System.out.println(e.getMessage());
   }
   }
   }
```

OUTPUT:

Please enter your roll number
-5
An exception is thrown
The number entered is not positive

Programs: Java Programs On Throws

Example 1

```
class Test
   {
   publicstaticvoid func() throws ArithmeticException {
   int num = 10 / 0;
   }
   publicstaticvoid main(String[] args) {
   func();
   }
   }
```

OUTPUT:

Exception in thread "main" java.lang.ArithmeticException: / by zero
at Test.func(Test.java:3)
at Test.main(Test.java:7)

Example 2

```
class Test {
    publicstaticvoid calculate()
    throws ArithmeticException, ArrayIndexOutOfBoundsException {
    int num = 10 / 0;
    // some code that might throw ArrayIndexOutOfBoundsException
    }
    publicstaticvoid main(String[] args) {
    try {
    calculate();
    } catch (ArithmeticException e) {
    System.out.println("Arithmetic Exception thrown");
    System.out.println(e.getMessage());
    } catch (ArrayIndexOutOfBoundsException e) {
    System.out.println("ArrayIndexOutOfBounds Exception thrown");
    System.out.println(e.getMessage());
    }
    }
    }
```

OUTPUT:

Programs: Java Programs on Arithmetic Exception thrown / by zero

Example 1

```
import java.io.*;
    class Test {
    publicstaticvoid calculate() throws IOException {
    thrownew IOException("IOException occurred");
    }
    publicstaticvoid main(String[] args) {
    try {
    calculate();
    } catch (IOException e) {
    System.out.println(e.getMessage());
    }
    }
    }
```

OUTPUT:

IOException occurred

Example 2

```
import java.io.*;
class Test {
publicstaticvoid func() throws IOException, ClassNotFoundException {
// statements which might throw IOException or ClassNotFoundException
}
publicstaticvoid main(String[] args) {
try {
func();
} catch (IOException e) {
System.out.println(e.getMessage());
}
}
}
```

OUTPUT:

```
Test.java:10: error: unreported exception ClassNotFoundException; must be caught or declared to be thrown
func();
^
1 error
```

CHAPTER TWELVE

Streams – Byte streams and Character streams

Program: Java Program Using I/O Streams

```
class HelloWorld
    {
    public static void main(String[] args)
    {
    System.out.println("Hello, World! Welcome to Java Programming");
    }
    }
```

OUTPUT:

Hello, World! Welcome to Java Programming

Program: Java Progam Using Byte Stream

//InputStream Using FileInputStream

```
import java.io.FileInputStream;
    import java.io.InputStream;
    class Main
    {
    public static void main(String args[]) {
    byte[] array = new byte[100];
    try {
    InputStream input = new FileInputStream("input.txt");
    System.out.println("Available bytes in the file: " + input.available());
    // Read byte from the input stream
    input.read(array);
    System.out.println("Data read from the file: ");
    // Convert byte array into string
    String data = new String(array);
    System.out.println(data);
    // Close the input stream
```

```
input.close();
} catch (Exception e) {
e.getStackTrace();
}
}
}
```

OUTPUT:

```
Available bytes in the file: 39
Data read from the file:
This is a line of text inside the file
```

Program: Java Program Using ByteArrayInputStream Class

//ByteArrayInputStream to read data

```
import java.io.ByteArrayInputStream;
public class Main
{
public static void main(String[] args)
{
// Creates an array of byte
byte[] array = {1, 2, 3, 4};
try
{
ByteArrayInputStream input = new ByteArrayInputStream(array);
System.out.print("The bytes read from the input stream: ");
for(int i= 0; i < array.length; i++)
{
// Reads the bytes
int data = input.read();
System.out.print(data + ", ");
}
input.close();
}
catch(Exception e)
{
e.getStackTrace();
}
}
}
```

OUTPUT:

```
The bytes read from the input stream: 1, 2, 3, 4,
```

Program: Java Program Using available() Method

```
//To get the number of available bytes in the input stream, we can use the available() method. For example,
public class Main
{
public static void main(String args[])
{
// Creates an array of bytes
byte[] array = { 1, 2, 3, 4 };
try
{
ByteArrayInputStream input = new ByteArrayInputStream(array);
// Returns the available number of bytes
System.out.println("Available bytes at the beginning: " + input.available());
// Reads 2 bytes from the input stream
input.read();
input.read();
// Returns the available number of bytes
System.out.println("Available bytes at the end: " + input.available());
input.close();
}
catch (Exception e)
{
e.getStackTrace();
}
}
}
```

OUTPUT:

Available bytes at the beginning: 4
Available bytes at the end: 2

Program: Java Program Using skip() Method

```
//To discard and skip the specified number of bytes, we can use the skip() method. For example,
import java.io.ByteArrayInputStream;
public class Main
{
public static void main(String args[])
{
// Create an array of bytes
byte[] array = { 1, 2, 3, 4 };
try
{
ByteArrayInputStream input = new ByteArrayInputStream(array);
// Using the skip() method
input.skip(2);
```

```
System.out.print("Input stream after skipping 2 bytes: ");
int data = input.read();
while (data != -1)
{
System.out.print(data + ", ");
data = input.read();
}
// close() method
input.close();
}
catch (Exception e)
{
e.getStackTrace();
}
}
}
```

OUTPUT:

Input stream after skipping 2 bytes: 3, 4,

Program: Java Program Using ObjectInputStream Class

```
//use the ObjectInputStream class to read objects written by the ObjectOutputStream class.
import java.io.FileInputStream;
import java.io.FileOutputStream;
import java.io.ObjectInputStream;
import java.io.ObjectOutputStream;
class Main
{
public static void main(String[] args)
{
int data1 = 5;
String data2 = "This is programiz";
try
{
FileOutputStream file = new FileOutputStream("file.txt");
ObjectOutputStream output = new ObjectOutputStream(file);
// Writing to the file using ObjectOutputStream
output.writeInt(data1);
output.writeObject(data2);
FileInputStream fileStream = new FileInputStream("file.txt");
// Creating an object input stream
ObjectInputStream objStream = new ObjectInputStream(fileStream);
//Using the readInt() method
System.out.println("Integer data :" + objStream.readInt());
// Using the readObject() method
System.out.println("String data: " + objStream.readObject());
```

```
output.close();
objStream.close();
}
catch (Exception e)
{
e.getStackTrace();
}
}
}
```

OUTPUT:

Integer data: 5
String data: This is programiz

Program: Java Program Using ObjectInputStream

```
import java.io.FileInputStream;
import java.io.FileOutputStream;
import java.io.ObjectInputStream;
import java.io.ObjectOutputStream;
import java.io.Serializable;
class Dog implements Serializable
{
String name;
String breed;
public Dog(String name, String breed)
{
this.name = name;
this.breed = breed;
}
}
class Main
{
public static void main(String[] args)
{
// Creates an object of Dog class
Dog dog = new Dog("Tyson", "Labrador");
try
{
FileOutputStream file = new FileOutputStream("file.txt");
// Creates an ObjectOutputStream
ObjectOutputStream output = new ObjectOutputStream(file);
// Writes objects to the output stream
output.writeObject(dog);
FileInputStream fileStream = new FileInputStream("file.txt");
// Creates an ObjectInputStream
ObjectInputStream input = new ObjectInputStream(fileStream);
```

```
// Reads the objects
Dog newDog = (Dog) input.readObject();
System.out.println("Dog Name: " + newDog.name);
System.out.println("Dog Breed: " + newDog.breed);
output.close();
input.close();
}
catch (Exception e)
{
e.getStackTrace();
}
}
}
```

OUTPUT:

```
Dog Name: Tyson
Dog Breed: Labrador
```

Program: Java Program ObjectInputStream Class

//Java ObjectInputStream

```
import java.io.FileInputStream;
import java.io.FileOutputStream;
import java.io.ObjectInputStream;
import java.io.ObjectOutputStream;
class Main
{
public static void main(String[] args)
{
int data1 = 5;
String data2 = "This is Java programming";
try
{
FileOutputStream file = new FileOutputStream("file.txt");
ObjectOutputStream output = new ObjectOutputStream(file);
// Writing to the file using ObjectOutputStream
output.writeInt(data1);
output.writeObject(data2);
FileInputStream fileStream = new FileInputStream("file.txt");
// Creating an object input stream
ObjectInputStream objStream = new ObjectInputStream(fileStream);
//Using the readInt() method
System.out.println("Integer data :" + objStream.readInt());
// Using the readObject() method
System.out.println("String data: " + objStream.readObject());
```

```
output.close();
objStream.close();
}
catch (Exception e)
{
e.getStackTrace();
}
}
}
```

OUTPUT:

Integer data: 5
String data: This is Java programming

Program: Java Program Using ObjectInputStream

```
import java.io.FileInputStream;
import java.io.FileOutputStream;
import java.io.ObjectInputStream;
import java.io.ObjectOutputStream;
import java.io.Serializable;
class Dog implements Serializable
{
String name;
String breed;
public Dog(String name, String breed)
{
this.name = name;
this.breed = breed;
}
}
class Main
{
public static void main(String[] args)
{
// Creates an object of Dog class
Dog dog = new Dog("Tyson", "Labrador");
try {
FileOutputStream file = new FileOutputStream("file.txt");
// Creates an ObjectOutputStream
ObjectOutputStream output = new ObjectOutputStream(file);
// Writes objects to the output stream
output.writeObject(dog);
FileInputStream fileStream = new FileInputStream("file.txt");
// Creates an ObjectInputStream
ObjectInputStream input = new ObjectInputStream(fileStream);
// Reads the objects
```

```
Dog newDog = (Dog) input.readObject();
System.out.println("Dog Name: " + newDog.name);
System.out.println("Dog Breed: " + newDog.breed);
output.close();
input.close();
}
catch (Exception e) {
e.getStackTrace();
}
}
}
```

OUTPUT:

```
Dog Name: Tyson
Dog Breed: Labrador
```

Program: Java Program Using FileInputStream Class

```
import java.io.FileInputStream;
public class Main
{
public static void main(String args[])
{
try
{
FileInputStream input = new FileInputStream("input.txt");
System.out.println("Data in the file: ");
// Reads the first byte
int i = input.read();
while(i != -1) {
System.out.print((char)i);
// Reads next byte from the file
i = input.read();
}
input.close();
}
catch(Exception e)
{
e.getStackTrace();
}
}
}
```

OUTPUT:

```
Data in the file:
This is a line of text inside the file.
```

Program: Java Program Using available() Method

```
import java.io.FileInputStream;
    public class Main
    {
    public static void main(String args[])
    {
    try
    {
    // Suppose, the input.txt file contains the following text
    // This is a line of text inside the file.
    FileInputStream input = new FileInputStream("input.txt");
    // Returns the number of available bytes
    System.out.println("Available bytes at the beginning: " + input.available());
    // Reads 3 bytes from the file
    input.read();
    input.read();
    input.read();
    // Returns the number of available bytes
    System.out.println("Available bytes at the end: " + input.available());
    input.close();
    }
    catch (Exception e)
    {
    e.getStackTrace();
    }
    }
    }
```

OUTPUT:

```
Available bytes at the beginning: 39
    Available bytes at the end: 36
```

Program: Java Program Using skip() Method

```
import java.io.FileInputStream;
    public class Main
    {
    public static void main(String args[])
    {
    try {
    // Suppose, the input.txt file contains the following text
    // This is a line of text inside the file.
    FileInputStream input = new FileInputStream("input.txt");
    // Skips the 5 bytes
    input.skip(5);
```

```
System.out.println("Input stream after skipping 5 bytes:");
// Reads the first byte
int i = input.read();
while (i != -1) {
System.out.print((char) i);
// Reads next byte from the file
i = input.read();
}
// close() method
input.close();
}
catch (Exception e)
{
e.getStackTrace();
}
}
}
```

OUTPUT:

Input Stream after skipping 5 bytes:
is a line of text inside the file.

Program: Java Program Using Java FileOutputStream Class

//FileOutputStream to write data to a File

```
import java.io.FileOutputStream;
public class Main
{
public static void main(String[] args)
{
String data = "This is a line of text inside the file.";
try
{
FileOutputStream output = new FileOutputStream("output.txt");
byte[] array = data.getBytes();
// Writes byte to the file
output.write(array);
output.close();
}
catch(Exception e)
{
e.getStackTrace();
}
}
}
```

Program: Java Program Using ByteArrayOutputStream Class

//ByteArrayOutputStream to write data

```
import java.io.ByteArrayOutputStream;
    class Main
    {
    public static void main(String[] args)
    {
    String data = "This is a line of text inside the string.";
    try
    {
    // Creates an output stream
    ByteArrayOutputStream out = new ByteArrayOutputStream();
    byte[] array = data.getBytes();
    // Writes data to the output stream
    out.write(array);
    // Retrieves data from the output stream in string format
    String streamData = out.toString();
    System.out.println("Output stream: " + streamData);
    out.close();
    }
    catch(Exception e)
    {
    e.getStackTrace();
    }
    }
    }
```

OUTPUT:

Output stream: This is a line of text inside the string.

Program: Java Program, Accessing Data from ByteArrayOutputStream

```
import java.io.ByteArrayOutputStream;
    class Main
    {
    public static void main(String[] args)
    {
    String data = "This is data.";
    try
    {
    // Creates an output stream
    ByteArrayOutputStream out = new ByteArrayOutputStream();
    // Writes data to the output stream
    out.write(data.getBytes());
```

```
// Returns an array of bytes
byte[] byteData = out.toByteArray();
System.out.print("Data using toByteArray(): ");
for(int i=0; i<byteData.length; i++)
{
System.out.print((char)byteData[i]);
}
// Returns a string
String stringData = out.toString();
System.out.println("\nData using toString(): " + stringData);
out.close();
}
catch(Exception e)
{
e.getStackTrace();
}
}
}
```

OUTPUT:

```
Data using toByteArray(): This is data.
Data using toString(): This is data.
```

Program: Java Program Using ObjectInputStream Class

//Example 1: Java ObjectInputStream

```
import java.io.FileInputStream;
import java.io.FileOutputStream;
import java.io.ObjectInputStream;
import java.io.ObjectOutputStream;
class Main
{
public static void main(String[] args)
{
int data1 = 5;
String data2 = "This is Java programming";
try
{
FileOutputStream file = new FileOutputStream("file.txt");
ObjectOutputStream output = new ObjectOutputStream(file);
// Writing to the file using ObjectOutputStream
output.writeInt(data1);
output.writeObject(data2);
FileInputStream fileStream = new FileInputStream("file.txt");
// Creating an object input stream
```

```
ObjectInputStream objStream = new ObjectInputStream(fileStream);
//Using the readInt() method
System.out.println("Integer data :" + objStream.readInt());
// Using the readObject() method
System.out.println("String data: " + objStream.readObject());
output.close();
objStream.close();
}
catch (Exception e)
{
e.getStackTrace();
}
}
}
```

OUTPUT:

```
Integer data: 5
String data: This is Java programming
```

Program: Java Program, Using ObjectInputStream

```
import java.io.FileInputStream;
import java.io.FileOutputStream;
import java.io.ObjectInputStream;
import java.io.ObjectOutputStream;
import java.io.Serializable;
class Computer implements Serializable
{
String name;
String brand;
public Dog(String name, String brand)
{
this.name = name;
this.breed = brand;
}
}
class Main
{
public static void main(String[] args)
{
// Creates an object of Computer class
Computer computer1 = new Computer("PC", "Samsung");
try
{
FileOutputStream file = new FileOutputStream("file.txt");
// Creates an ObjectOutputStream
ObjectOutputStream output = new ObjectOutputStream(file);
```

```
// Writes objects to the output stream
output.writeObject(computer);
FileInputStream fileStream = new FileInputStream("file.txt");
// Creates an ObjectInputStream
ObjectInputStream input = new ObjectInputStream(fileStream);
// Reads the objects
Computer newComputer = (Computer) input.readObject();
System.out.println("Computer Name: " + newComputer.name);
System.out.println("Computer Brand: " + newComputer.brand);
output.close();
input.close();
}
catch (Exception e)
{
e.getStackTrace();
}
}
}
```

OUTPUT:

```
Computer Name: PC
Computer Brand: Samsung
```

Program: Java Program Using ObjectOutputStream Class

//Sample Java ObjectOutputStream

```
import java.io.FileInputStream;
import java.io.FileOutputStream;
import java.io.ObjectInputStream;
import java.io.ObjectOutputStream;
class Main
{
public static void main(String[] args)
{
int data1 = 5;
String data2 = "This is Java programming";
try
{
FileOutputStream file = new FileOutputStream("file.txt");
// Creates an ObjectOutputStream
ObjectOutputStream output = new ObjectOutputStream(file);
// writes objects to output stream
output.writeInt(data1);
output.writeObject(data2);
// Reads data using the ObjectInputStream
```

```
FileInputStream fileStream = new FileInputStream("file.txt");
ObjectInputStream objStream = new ObjectInputStream(fileStream);
System.out.println("Integer data :" + objStream.readInt());
System.out.println("String data: " + objStream.readObject());
output.close();
objStream.close();
}
catch (Exception e)
{
e.getStackTrace();
}
}
}
```

OUTPUT:

Integer data: 5
String data: This is Java programming

Program: Java Program Using ObjectOutputStream

```
import java.io.FileInputStream;
import java.io.FileOutputStream;
import java.io.ObjectInputStream;
import java.io.ObjectOutputStream;
import java.io.Serializable;
class Dog implements Serializable
{
String name;
String breed;
public Dog(String name, String breed)
{
this.name = name;
this.breed = breed;
}
}
class Main
{
public static void main(String[] args)
{
// Creates an object of Dog class
Dog dog1 = new Dog("Babu", "GermanShepherd");
try {
FileOutputStream fileOut = new FileOutputStream("file.txt");
// Creates an ObjectOutputStream
ObjectOutputStream objOut = new ObjectOutputStream(fileOut);
// Writes objects to the output stream
objOut.writeObject(dog1);
```

```
// Reads the object
FileInputStream fileIn = new FileInputStream("file.txt");
ObjectInputStream objIn = new ObjectInputStream(fileIn);
// Reads the objects
Dog newDog = (Dog) objIn.readObject();
System.out.println("Dog Name: " + newDog.name);
System.out.println("Dog Breed: " + newDog.breed);
objOut.close();
objIn.close();
}
catch (Exception e)
{
e.getStackTrace();
}
}
}
```

Output

```
Dog Name: Babu
Dog Breed: GermanShepherd
```

Program: Java Program Using BufferedInputStream Class

```
import java.io.BufferedInputStream;
import java.io.FileInputStream;
class Main
{
public static void main(String[] args)
{
try
{
// Creates a FileInputStream
FileInputStream file = new FileInputStream("input.txt");
// Creates a BufferedInputStream
BufferedInputStream input = new BufferedInputStream(file);
// Reads first byte from file
int i = input .read();
while (i != -1)
{
System.out.print((char) i);
// Reads next byte from the file
i = input.read();
}
input.close();
}
catch (Exception e)
{
e.getStackTrace();
}
```

```
}
}
```

OUTPUT:

This is a line of text inside the file.

Program: Java Program Using available() Method

```
import java.io.FileInputStream;
import java.io.BufferedInputStream;
public class Main
{
public static void main(String args[])
{
try
{
// Suppose, the input.txt file contains the following text
// This is a line of text inside the file.
FileInputStream file = new FileInputStream("input.txt");
// Creates a BufferedInputStream
BufferedInputStream buffer = new BufferedInputStream(file);
// Returns the available number of bytes
System.out.println("Available bytes at the beginning: " + buffer.available());
// Reads bytes from the file
buffer.read();
buffer.read();
buffer.read();
// Returns the available number of bytes
System.out.println("Available bytes at the end: " + buffer.available());
buffer.close();
}
catch (Exception e)
{
e.getStackTrace();
}
}
}
```

OUTPUT:

Available bytes at the beginning: 39
Available bytes at the end: 36

Program: Java Program Using skip() Method

```
import java.io.FileInputStream;
import java.io.BufferedInputStream;
```

```
public class Main
{
public static void main(String args[])
{
try
{
// Suppose, the input.txt file contains the following text
// This is a line of text inside the file.
FileInputStream file = new FileInputStream("input.txt");
// Creates a BufferedInputStream
BufferedInputStream buffer = new BufferedInputStream(file);
// Skips the 5 bytes
buffer.skip(5);
System.out.println("Input stream after skipping 5 bytes:");
// Reads the first byte from input stream
int i = buffer.read();
while (i != -1)
{
System.out.print((char) i);
// Reads next byte from the input stream
i = buffer.read();
}
// Closes the input stream
buffer.close();
}
catch (Exception e)
{
e.getStackTrace();
}
}
}
```

OUTPUT:

Input stream after skipping 5 bytes: is a line of text inside the file.

Program: Java Program Using BufferedOutputStream Class

//Example: BufferedOutputStream to write data to a File

```
import java.io.FileOutputStream;
import java.io.BufferedOutputStream;
public class Main
{
public static void main(String[] args)
{
String data = "This is a line of text inside the file";
try
{
```

```
// Creates a FileOutputStream
FileOutputStream file = new FileOutputStream("output.txt");
// Creates a BufferedOutputStream
BufferedOutputStream output = new BufferedOutputStream(file);
byte[] array = data.getBytes();
// Writes data to the output stream
output.write(array);
output.close();
}
catch (Exception e)
{
e.getStackTrace();
}
}
}
```

OUTPUT:

This is a line of text inside the file.

Program: Java Program Using flush() Method

```
import java.io.FileOutputStream;
import java.io.BufferedOutputStream;
public class Main
{
public static void main(String[] args)
{
String data = "This is a demo of the flush method";
try
{
// Creates a FileOutputStream
FileOutputStream file = new FileOutputStream(" flush.txt");
// Creates a BufferedOutputStream
BufferedOutputStream buffer = new BufferedOutputStream(file);
// Writes data to the output stream
buffer.write(data.getBytes());
// Flushes data to the destination
buffer.flush();
System.out.println("Data is flushed to the file.");
buffer.close();
}
catch(Exception e)
{
e.getStackTrace();
}
}
}
```

OUTPUT:

Data is flushed to the file.

Program: Java Program Using Java PrintStream Class

```
//Example: print() method with System class
    class Main
    {
    public static void main(String[] args)
    {
    String data = "Hello World.";
    System.out.print(data);
    }
    }
```

OUTPUT:

Hello World.

Program: Java Program Using print() method with PrintStream class

```
import java.io.PrintStream;
    class Main
    {
    public static void main(String[] args)
    {
    String data = "This is a text inside the file.";
    try
    {
    PrintStream output = new PrintStream("output.txt");
    output.print(data);
    output.close();
    }
    catch(Exception e)
    {
    e.getStackTrace();
    }
    }
    }
```

OUTPUT:

This is a text inside the file.

Program: Java Program Using printf() method with PrintStream

```
import java.io.PrintStream;
    class Main
    {
    public static void main(String[] args)
    {
    try
    {
    PrintStream output = new PrintStream("output.txt");
    int age = 25;
    output.printf("I am %d years old.", age);
    output.close();
    }
    catch(Exception e)
    {
    e.getStackTrace();
    }
    }
    }
```

OUTPUT:

I am 25 years old.

Program: Java Program Using printf() Method Using PrintStream

```
import java.io.PrintStream;
    class Main
    {
    public static void main(String[] args)
    {
    try
    {
    PrintStream output = new PrintStream("output.txt");
    int age = 25;
    output.printf("I am %d years old.", age);
    output.close();
    }
    catch(Exception e)
    {
    e.getStackTrace();
    }
    }
    }
```

OUTPUT:

I am 25 years old.

Program: Java Program to Create Files

//Example: Create a new File

```
// importing the File class
import java.io.File;
class Main
{
public static void main(String[] args)
{
// create a file object for the current location
File file = new File("newFile.txt");
try
{
// trying to create a file based on the object
boolean value = file.createNewFile();
if (value)
{
System.out.println("The new file is created.");
}
else
{
System.out.println("The file already exists.");
}
}
catch(Exception e)
{
e.getStackTrace();
}
}
}
```

OUTPUT:

The new file is created.
The new file is created.

Program: Java Program to Read Files

//To read data from the file, we can use subclasses of either InputStream or Reader.

//Example To Read a file using FileReader

```
// importing the FileReader class
import java.io.FileReader;
class Main
{
public static void main(String[] args)
{
```

```
char[] array = new char[100];
try
{
// Creates a reader using the FileReader
FileReader input = new FileReader("input.txt");
// Reads characters
input.read(array);
System.out.println("Data in the file:");
System.out.println(array);
// Closes the reader
input.close();
}
catch(Exception e)
{
e.getStackTrace();
}
}
}
```

OUTPUT:

Data in the file:
This is a line of text inside the file.

Program: Java Program to Write to Files

```
// importing the FileWriter class
import java.io.FileWriter;
class Main
{
public static void main(String args[])
{
String data = "This is the data in the output file";
try
{
// Creates a Writer using FileWriter
FileWriter output = new FileWriter("output.txt");
// Writes string to the file
output.write(data);
System.out.println("Data is written to the file.");
// Closes the writer
output.close();
}
catch (Exception e)
{
e.getStackTrace();
}
}
```

```
}
```

OUTPUT:

Data is written to the file.

Program: Java Program to Delete Files

```
import java.io.File;
    class Main
    {
    public static void main(String[] args)
    {
    // creates a file object
    File file = new File("file.txt");
    // deletes the file
    boolean value = file.delete();
    if(value) {
    System.out.println("The File is deleted.");
    }
    else {
    System.out.println("The File is not deleted.");
    }
    }
    }
```

OUTPUT:

The File is deleted.

CHAPTER THIRTEEN

Multi-threading and multitasking

Java Example: Execute a single task by multiple threads

```
public class SingleTaskMultipleThreads extends Thread
    {
    public void run()
    {
    System.out.println("Executing task");
    }
    public static void main(String[] args)
    {
    SingleTaskMultipleThreads t1 = new SingleTaskMultipleThreads();
    SingleTaskMultipleThreads t2 = new SingleTaskMultipleThreads();
    SingleTaskMultipleThreads t3 = new SingleTaskMultipleThreads();
    t1.start();
    t2.start();
    t3.start();
    }
    }
```

OUTPUT:

```
Executing task
    Executing task
    Executing task
```

Program: Java Program to Create an Instance of the Thread classand Pass the Anonymous Object of the Main Class

```
public class SingleTaskExecution implements Runnable
    {
    public static void main(String[] args)
    {
    Thread th1 = new Thread(new SingleTaskExecution());
    Thread th2 = new Thread(new SingleTaskExecution());
    th1.start();
    th2.start();
    }
```

```
@Override
public void run()
{
System.out.println("Executing task");
}
}
```

OUTPUT:

```
Executing task
Executing task
```

Program: Java Program for Executing Multiple Tasks Using Multiple Threads – Multitasking

```
class Task1 extends Thread
{
public void run()
{
System.out.println("Executing task 1");
}
}
class Task2 extends Thread
{
public void run()
{
System.out.println("Executing task 2");
}
}
public class MultitaskingDemo
{
public static void main(String[] args)
{
Task1 t1 = new Task1();
Task2 t2 = new Task2();
t1.start();
t2.start();
}
}
```

OUTPUT:

```
Executing task 1
Executing task 2
```

Program: Java Program, Example of Multitasking in Java by Implementing the Runnable interface

```
class SimpleTask1 implements Runnable
```

```
{
@Override
public void run()
{
System.out.println("Executing task1");
}
}
class SimpleTask2 implements Runnable
{
@Override
public void run()
{
System.out.println("Executing task2");
}
}
public class MultiTaskingEx
{
public static void main(String[] args)
{
Thread th1 = new Thread(new SimpleTask1());
Thread th2 = new Thread(new SimpleTask2());
th1.start();
th2.start();
}
}
```

OUTPUT:

Executing task1
Executing task2

Java Program for Demonstrating Thread States

```
//FileName: ThreadState.java
// ABC class implements the interface Runnable
class ABC implements Runnable
{
publicvoid run()
{
// try-catch block
try
{
// moving thread t2 to the state timed waiting
Thread.sleep(100);
}
catch (InterruptedException ie)
{
ie.printStackTrace();
```

```
}
System.out.println("The state of thread t1 while it invoked the method join() on thread t2 -"+
ThreadState.t1.getState());
// try-catch block
try
{
Thread.sleep(200);
}
catch (InterruptedException ie)
{
ie.printStackTrace();
}
}
}
// ThreadState class implements the interface Runnable
publicclass ThreadState implements Runnable
{
publicstatic Thread t1;
publicstatic ThreadState obj;
// main method
publicstaticvoid main(String argvs[])
{
// creating an object of the class ThreadState
obj = new ThreadState();
t1 = new Thread(obj);
// thread t1 is spawned
// The thread t1 is currently in the NEW state.
System.out.println("The state of thread t1 after spawning it - " + t1.getState());
// invoking the start() method on
// the thread t1
t1.start();
// thread t1 is moved to the Runnable state
System.out.println("The state of thread t1 after invoking the method start() on it - " + t1.getState());
}
publicvoid run()
{
ABC myObj = new ABC();
Thread t2 = new Thread(myObj);
// thread t2 is created and is currently in the NEW state.
System.out.println("The state of thread t2 after spawning it - "+ t2.getState());
t2.start();
// thread t2 is moved to the runnable state
System.out.println("the state of thread t2 after calling the method start() on it - " + t2.getState());
// try-catch block for the smooth flow of the program
try
{
// moving the thread t1 to the state timed waiting
Thread.sleep(200);
```

```
}
catch (InterruptedException ie)
{
ie.printStackTrace();
}
System.out.println("The state of thread t2 after invoking the method sleep() on it - "+ t2.getState() );
// try-catch block for the smooth flow of the program
try
{
// waiting for thread t2 to complete its execution
t2.join();
}
catch (InterruptedException ie)
{
ie.printStackTrace();
}
System.out.println("The state of thread t2 when it has completed it's execution - " + t2.getState());
}
}
```

OUTPUT:

The state of thread t1 after spawning it - NEW
The state of thread t1 after invoking the method start() on it - RUNNABLE
The state of thread t2 after spawning it - NEW
the state of thread t2 after calling the method start() on it - RUNNABLE
The state of thread t1 while it invoked the method join() on thread t2 -TIMED_WAITING
The state of thread t2 after invoking the method sleep() on it - TIMED_WAITING
The state of thread t2 when it has completed it's execution - TERMINATED

Program: Java Thread Example by Extending Thread class

```
//FileName: Multi.java
class Multi extends Thread
{
publicvoid run()
{
System.out.println("thread is running...");
}
publicstaticvoid main(String args[])
{
Multi t1=new Multi();
t1.start();
}
}
```

OUTPUT:

thread is running...

Program: Java Thread Example by implementing Runnable interface

```
//FileName: Multi3.java
    class Multi3 implements Runnable
{
    publicvoid run()
    {
    System.out.println("thread is running...");
    }
    publicstaticvoid main(String args[])
    {
    Multi3 m1=new Multi3();
    Thread t1 =new Thread(m1); // Using the constructor Thread(Runnable r)
    t1.start();
    }
    }
```

OUTPUT:

thread is running...

Program: Java Program Using the Thread Class: Thread(String Name)

```
//We can directly use the Thread class to spawn new threads using the constructors defined above.
    //FileName: MyThread1.java
    publicclass MyThread1
    {
    // Main method
    publicstaticvoid main(String argvs[])
    {
    // creating an object of the Thread class using the constructor Thread(String name)
    Thread t= new Thread("My first thread");
    // the start() method moves the thread to the active state
    t.start();
    // getting the thread name by invoking the getName() method
    String str = t.getName();
    System.out.println(str);
    }
    }
```

OUTPUT:

My first thread

Program: Java Program Using the Thread Class: Thread(Runnable r, String name)

//Observe the following program.

```
//FileName: MyThread2.java
publicclass MyThread2 implements Runnable
{
publicvoid run()
{
System.out.println("Now the thread is running ...");
}
// main method
publicstaticvoid main(String argvs[])
{
// creating an object of the class MyThread2
Runnable r1 = new MyThread2();
// creating an object of the class Thread using Thread(Runnable r, String name)
Thread th1 = new Thread(r1, "My new thread");
// the start() method moves the thread to the active state
th1.start();
// getting the thread name by invoking the getName() method
String str = th1.getName();
System.out.println(str);
}
}
```

OUTPUT:

```
My new thread
Now the thread is running ...
```

Program: Java Program Thread Scheduler in Java

Example of the sleep() method in Java : on the custom thread

```
//FileName: TestSleepMethod1.java
class TestSleepMethod1 extends Thread
{
publicvoid run()
{
for(int i=1;i<5;i++)
{
// the thread will sleep for the 500 milli seconds
try
{
Thread.sleep(500);
}
catch(InterruptedException e)
{
System.out.println(e);
```

```
}
System.out.println(i);
}
}
publicstaticvoid main(String args[])
{
TestSleepMethod1 t1=new TestSleepMethod1();
TestSleepMethod1 t2=new TestSleepMethod1();
t1.start();
t2.start();
}
}
```

OUTPUT:

```
1
1
2
2
3
3
4
4
```

Program: Java Program Example of the sleep() Method in Java : On The Main Thread

```
//FileName: TestSleepMethod2.java
// important import statements
import java.lang.Thread;
import java.io.*;
publicclass TestSleepMethod2
{
// main method
publicstaticvoid main(String argvs[])
{
try
{
for (int j = 0; j < 5; j++)
{
// The main thread sleeps for the 1000 milliseconds, which is 1 sec
// whenever the loop runs
Thread.sleep(1000);
// displaying the value of the variable
System.out.println(j);
}
}
catch (Exception expn)
{
```

```
// catching the exception
System.out.println(expn);
}
}
}
```

OUTPUT:

```
0
1
2
3
4
```

Program: Java Program Example of the sleep() Method in Java:

//The following example throws the exception IllegalArguementException //when the time for sleeping is negative.

FileName: TestSleepMethod3.java

```
// important import statements
import java.lang.Thread;
import java.io.*;
publicclass TestSleepMethod3
{
// main method
publicstaticvoid main(String argvs[])
{
// we can also use throws keyword followed by
// exception name for throwing the exception
try
{
for (int j = 0; j < 5; j++)
{
// it throws the exception IllegalArgumentException
// as the time is -ive which is -100
Thread.sleep(-100);
// displaying the variable's value
System.out.println(j);
}
}
catch (Exception expn)
{
// the exception iscaught here
System.out.println(expn);
}
}
```

```
}
```

OUTPUT:

```
1
1
2
2
3
3
4
4
```

Program: Java Program Example of the sleep() Method in Java: When the sleeping time is -ive

```
//The following example throws the exception IllegalArguementException
//when the time for sleeping is negative.
//FileName: TestSleepMethod3.java
// important import statements
import java.lang.Thread;
import java.io.*;
publicclass TestSleepMethod3
{
// main method
publicstaticvoid main(String argvs[])
{
// we can also use throws keyword followed by
// exception name for throwing the exception
try
{
for (int j = 0; j < 5; j++)
{
// it throws the exception IllegalArgumentException
// as the time is -ive which is -100
Thread.sleep(-100);
// displaying the variable's value
System.out.println(j);
}
}
catch (Exception expn)
{
// the exception iscaught here
System.out.println(expn);
}
}
}
```

OUTPUT:

java.lang.IllegalArgumentException: timeout value is negative

Program: Java Program Using Threads and Exception

```
publicclass TestThreadTwice1 extends Thread{
    publicvoid run(){
    System.out.println("running...");
    }
    publicstaticvoid main(String args[]){
    TestThreadTwice1 t1=new TestThreadTwice1();
    t1.start();
    t1.start();
    }
    }
```

OUTPUT:

running

Program: Java Program Using Exception in thread "main" java.lang.IllegalThreadStateException

```
//What if we call Java run() method directly instead start() method?
    //Each thread starts in a separate call stack.
    //Invoking the run() method from the main thread, the run() method goes onto the current
    //call stack rather than at the beginning of a new call stack.
    //FileName: TestCallRun1.java
    class TestCallRun1 extends Thread
    {
    publicvoid run(){
    System.out.println("running...");
    }
    publicstaticvoid main(String args[])
    {
    TestCallRun1 t1=new TestCallRun1();
    t1.run();//fine, but does not start a separate call stack
    }
    }
```

OUTPUT:

running...

Printed by Libri Plureos GmbH in Hamburg,
Germany